WHAT EVERYONE SHOULD KNOW ABOUT
ECONOMICS AND PROSPERITY

James D. Gwartney and Richard L. Stroup

Photography Credits © 1993

Cover design: Kromhout & Kromhout Visual Design, Tallahassee, FL; cover photo: "World Map"—Uniphoto Picture Agency, Washington, DC; photo, p.10: "Robotics"— C.J. Howard, FPG International Corp., New York, NY; photos, p.16: "Farming"—1) John Colwell, Grant Heilman Photography Inc., Lititz, PA, 2) Grant Heilman, 3) Grant Heilman; photo, p.66: "Hong Kong Harbor"—Uniphoto Picture Agency. Special thanks to Amy Gwartney for the remaining photography.

ISBN 0-9653054-0-6

TABLE OF CONTENTS

Page

Introduction

Why should you read this book?

We realize that your time is valuable. Most of you do not want to spend a lot of time learning new terms, memorizing formulas, or mastering details that are important only to professional economists. What you want are the insights of economics that really matter—those that will help you make better personal choices and enhance your understanding of our complex world. And you want those insights to be presented in a concise, organized, and readable manner, with a minimum of economics *jargon*. This short book attempts to meet both of these objectives.

We think you can profit from this book regardless of your current knowledge of economics. If you are a beginner, this book will introduce you to a few basic economic principles that to a large degree merely reflect common sense. These concepts, however, are powerful tools. When making decisions, they will help you develop your thoughts logically and view the central issues more clearly. They will also enhance your ability to differentiate between sound arguments and economic nonsense.

If you are a student of economics or business, this book will help you pull together the "big picture." After 30 years of teaching college economics, the authors are painfully aware of two points: (1) students often miss important points because they are busy with extraneous graphs, formulas, and mathematical details and (2) they do not retain much of what is taught in their college economics courses. The information encapsulated in this book will challenge college students to think more seriously about the really important implications of economics—knowledge that will make a difference long after their final exam in economics is a faded memory.

Finally, even if you are a business executive or a policymaker, we believe you will find this book informative. However experienced you may be in your particular area, you may not fully appreciate how all the pieces of the economic puzzle fit together. This is often the case with people in both business and government. They know their job, but they have not thought very seriously about how political rules and policies influence the broader economic health of people and nations.

Studies indicate that we are a nation of economic illiterates. In a democratic setting, the consequences of economic illiteracy can be disastrous. People who do not understand the sources of economic prosperity are susceptible to schemes that conflict with the attainment of that prosperity. A nation of economic illiterates is unlikely to remain prosperous for very long. The basic principles explained in this book will help you better understand what types of economic arrangements work and why some nations prosper while others stagnate or even regress. As a result, you will be able to make wiser choices and become a better citizen.

Acknowledgements

The authors would like to thank the following people for helpful comments on earlier drafts of this book: Ljubisa Adamovic', Terry Anderson, John W. Cooper, Jack Fay, Randall Holcombe, Tom Palmer, Judd W. Patton, Scott W. Rasmussen, Ronald H. Salter, Jane S. Shaw, Russell S. Sobel, Carol Strauss, and Sharon Watson. They would also like to express their appreciation to the Philip M. McKenna Foundation and the Earhart Foundation for funding which facilitated the project and to Valerie N. Colvin for her excellent work on both word-processing and the design.

PART I:
Ten Key Elements of
Economics

TEN KEY ELEMENTS OF ECONOMICS

1. Incentives Matter.

2. There is No Such Thing as a Free Lunch.

3. Voluntary Exchange Promotes Economic Progress.

4. Transaction Costs are an Obstacle to Exchange; Reducing This Obstacle Will Help Promote Economic Progress.

5. Increases in Real Income are Dependent Upon Increases in Real Output.

6. The Four Sources of Income Growth are (a) Improvements in Worker Skills, (b) Capital Formation, (c) Technological Advancements, and (d) Better Economic Organization.

7. Income is Compensation Derived from the Provision of Services to Others. People Earn Income by Helping Others.

8. Profits Direct Businesses Toward Activities that Increase Wealth.

9. The "Invisible Hand" Principle—Market Prices Bring Personal Self-interest and the General Welfare into Harmony.

10. Ignoring Secondary Effects and Long-term Consequences is the Most Common Source of Error in Economics.

1. Incentives Matter.

All economic theory is based on the postulate that changes in incentives influence human behavior in a predictable manner. Personal benefits and costs influence our choices. If the benefits derived from an option increase, people will be more likely to choose it. Conversely, if the personal costs of an option increase, people will be less likely to choose it.

This basic postulate of economics is a powerful tool because its application is so widespread. Incentives affect behavior in virtually all aspects of our lives, ranging from market activities to household decision-making to political choices.

In the marketplace, the basic postulate indicates that, if the price of a good increases, consumers will buy less of it; producers, on the other hand, will supply more of it since the price increase makes it more profitable to produce the good. Both buyers and sellers respond to incentives. Market prices will bring their actions into harmony. If the quantity buyers want to purchase exceeds the quantity sellers are willing to provide, price will rise. The higher price will discourage consumption and encourage production of the good or service, bringing amount demanded and amount supplied into balance. Alternatively, if consumers are unwilling to purchase the current output of a good, inventories will accumulate and there will be downward pressure on price. In turn, the lower price will encourage consumption and retard production until the amount demanded by consumers is once again in balance with production of the good. Markets work because both buyers and sellers alter their behavior in response to changes in incentives.

3

Of course, this process does not work instanteously. It will take time for buyers to respond fully to a change in price. Similarly, it will take time for producers to build an additional plant in response to a price increase or reduce production if price declines. Nonetheless, the implications are clear—market prices will coordinate the actions of both buyers and sellers and bring them into harmony.

The response of buyers and sellers to the higher gasoline prices of the 1970s illustrates the importance of incentives. As gasoline prices rose, consumers eliminated less essential trips and did more car pooling. Gradually, they shifted to smaller, more fuel-efficient cars in order to reduce their gasoline consumption still further. At the same time, petroleum suppliers in the United States increased their drilling, used a water flooding technique to recover more oil from existing wells, and searched more intensely for new oil fields. By the early 1980s, this combination of factors was placing downward pressure on the price of crude oil.

Incentives also influence political choices. The person who shops in the supermarket is the same person who shops among political alternatives. In most cases, voters are more likely to support political candidates and policies that provide them with net personal benefits. Conversely, they will tend to oppose political options when the personal costs are high relative to the benefits provided.

The basic postulate of economics—that incentives matter—is just as applicable under socialism as it is under capitalism. For example, in the former Soviet Union, managers and employees of glass plants were at one time rewarded according to the tons of sheet glass produced. Not surprisingly, most plants produced sheet glass so thick that one could hardly see through it. The rules were changed so that the managers were rewarded according to the square meters of glass produced. The results were predictable. Under the new rules, Soviet firms produced

4

glass so thin that it was easily broken. Changes in incentives influence actions under all forms of economic organization.

Some critics have charged that economic analysis only helps explain the actions of self-centered, greedy materialists. This view is false. People act for a variety of reasons, some selfish and some humanitarian. The basic postulate of economics applies to both the altruist and egotist. The choices of both will be influenced by changes in personal costs and benefits. For example, both the altruist and the egotist will be more likely to attempt the rescue of a small child in a three-foot swimming pool than in the rapid currents approaching Niagara Falls. Similarly, both are more likely to give a needy person their hand-me-downs rather than their best clothes. Incentives influence the choices of both.

2. There is No Such Thing as a Free Lunch.

Scarcity constrains us. The reality of life on our planet is that productive resources are limited, while human desires for goods and services are virtually unlimited. Since we cannot have as much of everything as we would like, we are forced to choose among alternatives.

When resources are used to produce good A, say a shopping center, the action diverts resources away from the production of other goods that are also desired. The cost of the shopping center is the highest valued bundle of other goods that could have been produced and consumed, but now must be sacrificed, because the required resources were used instead to produce the shopping center. The use of resources to produce one thing reduces their availability to produce other things. Thus, the use of scarce resources always involves a cost; there is no such thing as a free lunch.

Costs play a vitally important function: they help us balance our desire for more of a good against our desire for more of *other* goods that could be produced instead. If we do not consider these costs, we will end up using scarce resources to produce the wrong things—goods that we do not value as much as other things that we might have produced.

In a market economy, consumer demand and producer costs perform this balancing function. In essence, the demand for a product is the voice of consumers instructing firms to produce a good. In order to produce the good, however, resources must be bid away from their alternative uses—primarily the production of other goods. Producers incur costs when they bid resources away from the production of other goods. These costs of production represent the voice of consumers saying that *other goods* that could be produced with the resources are also desired.

6

Producers have a strong incentive to supply those goods that can be sold for as much or more than their production costs. This is another way of saying that producers will tend to supply those goods that consumers value most relative to their production costs.

Of course, a good can be provided free to an individual or group if others foot the bill. But this merely shifts the costs; it does not reduce them. Politicians often speak of "free education," "free medical care," or "free housing". This terminology is deceptive. None of these things are free. Scarce resources are required to produce each of them. For example, the buildings, labor, and other resources used to produce schooling could be used instead to produce more food, recreation, entertainment, or other goods. The cost of the schooling is the value of those goods that must now be given up because the resources required for their production were instead used to produce schooling. Governments may be able to shift costs, but they cannot avoid them. The "scarce resources have a cost" concept applies to all.

With the passage of time, of course, we may be able to discover better ways of doing things and improve our knowledge about how to transform scarce resources into desired goods and services. Clearly, this has been the case. During the last 250 years, we have been able to relax the grip of scarcity and improve our quality of life. However, this does not change the fundamental point—we still confront the reality of scarcity. The use of more labor, machines, and natural resources to produce one good forces us to give up other goods that might otherwise have been produced.

3. Voluntary Exchange Promotes Economic Progress.

Mutual gain is the foundation of trade. Parties agree to an exchange because they anticipate that it will improve their well-being. The motivation for market exchange is summed up in the phrase, "If you do something good for me, I will do something good for you." Trade is productive; it permits each of the trading partners to get more of what they want.

There are three major reasons why trade is productive—why it increases the wealth of people. *First, trade channels goods and services to those who value them most.* A good or service does not have value just because it exists. Material things are not wealth until they are in the hands of someone who values them. The preferences, knowledge, and goals of people vary widely. Thus, a good that is virtually worthless to one may be a precious gem to another. For example, a highly technical book on electronics that is of no value to an art collector may be worth hundreds of dollars to an engineer. Similarly, a painting that is unappreciated by an engineer may be an object of great value to an art collector. Therefore, a voluntary exchange that moves the electronics book to the engineer and the painting to the art collector will increase the value of both goods. Simultaneously, the exchange will increase the wealth of both trading partners and the nation because it moves goods from people who value them less to people who value them more.

Second, exchange permits trading partners to gain from specializing in the production of those things they do best. Specialization allows us to expand total output. A group of individuals, regions, or nations will be able to produce a larger output when each specializes in the production of goods and services it can provide at a low cost, and uses its sales revenue to trade for desired goods it can provide only at a high cost. Economists refer to this principle as the law of comparative advantage.

In many ways, gains from trade and specialization are common sense. Examples abound. Trade permits a skilled carpenter to specialize in the production of frame housing while trading the earnings from housing sales to purchase food, clothing, automobiles, and thousands of other goods that the carpenter is not so skilled at producing. Similarly, trade allows Canadian farmers to specialize in the production of wheat and use the revenue from wheat sales to buy Brazilian coffee, a commodity that the Canadians could produce only at a high cost. Simultaneously, it is cheaper for Brazilians to use their resources to grow coffee and trade the revenues for Canadian wheat. Total output is enlarged and both trading partners gain.

Third, voluntary exchange permits us to realize gains derived from cooperative effort, division of labor, and the adoption of large-scale production methods. In the absence of exchange, productive activity would be limited to the individual household. Self-sufficiency and small-scale production would be the rule. Exchange permits us to have a much wider market for our output, and thus enables us to separate production processes into a series of specific operations in order to plan for large production runs—actions which often lead to enormous increases in output per worker.

Adam Smith, the "father of economics," stressed the importance of gains from the division of labor more than 200 years ago. Observing the operation of a pin manufacturer, Smith noted that the production of the pins was broken into "about eighteen distinct operations," each performed by specific workers. When the workers each specialized in a productive function, they were able to

Modern production of a good like a pencil or an automobile often involves specialization, division of labor, large-scale production methods, and the cooperation of literally tens of thousands of people. Gains from these sources are dependent upon exchange.

produce 4,800 pins *per worker* each day. Without specialization and division of labor, Smith doubted an individual worker would have been able to produce even 20 pins per day.

Specialization permits individuals to take advantage of the diversity in their abilities and skills. It also enables employers to assign tasks to the workers who are more able to accomplish them. Even more importantly, the division of labor lets us adopt complex, large-scale production techniques unthinkable for an individual household. Without exchange, however, these gains would be lost.

4. Transaction Costs are an Obstacle to Exchange; Reducing This Obstacle Will Help Promote Economic Progress.

Voluntary exchange is productive because it promotes social cooperation and helps us get more of what we want. However, exchange is also costly. The time, effort, and other resources necessary to search out, negotiate, and conclude an exchange are called transaction costs. Transaction costs are an obstacle to the creation of wealth. They limit both our productive capacity and the realization of gains from mutually advantageous trades.

Transaction costs are sometimes high because of physical obstacles, such as oceans, rivers, marshes, and mountains. In these cases, investment in roads and improvements in transportation and communications can reduce them. In other instances, transaction costs may be high because of man-made obstacles, such as taxes, licensing requirements, government regulations, price controls, tariffs, or quotas. But regardless of whether the roadblocks are physical or man-made, high transaction costs reduce the potential gains from trade. Conversely, reductions in transaction costs increase the gains from trade and thereby promote economic progress.

People who provide trading partners with information and services that help them arrange trades and make better choices are providing something valuable. Such specialists or middlemen include real estate agents, stockbrokers, automobile dealers, publishers of classified ads, and a wide variety of merchants.

Often, people believe that middlemen are unnecessary— that they merely increase the price of goods without providing benefits to either the buyer or the seller. Once we recognize that transaction costs are an obstacle to trade, it is easy to see the fallacy of this view. Consider the grocer who, in essence, provides middleman services that make it cheaper and more convenient for producers and consumers of food products to deal with each other. Think of the time and effort that would be involved in preparing even a single meal if shoppers had to deal directly with farmers when purchasing vegetables; citrus growers when buying fruit; dairy operators if they wanted butter, milk, or cheese; and a rancher or a fisherman if they wanted to serve beef or fish. Grocers make these contacts for consumers, transport and sell all of the items in a convenient shopping location, and maintain reliable inventories. The services of grocers and other middlemen reduce transaction costs and make it easier for potential buyers and sellers to realize gains from trade. These services increase the volume of trade and thereby promote economic progress.

5. Increases in Real Income are Dependent Upon Increases in Real Output.

A higher income and standard of living are dependent upon higher productivity and output. There is a direct relationship between a nation's per capita income and its per capita output. In essence, output and income are opposite sides of the same coin. Output is the value of the goods and services produced, as measured by the prices paid by purchasers. Income is the revenue paid to the people (including the entrepreneur's residual revenue), who supply the resources that generate the output. This too, must equal the sale price of the good.

Consider the following example: suppose that a construction company hires workers and purchases other resources, such as lumber, nails, and bricks, to produce output—in this case, a home. When the home is sold to a buyer, the sale price is a measure of output. Simultaneously, the sum of the payments to the workers, suppliers of the other resources, and the residual income received by the construction company (which may be either positive or negative) is a measure of income. Both the output and income add up to the sale price of the good, which represents the value of what was produced.

Once the linkage between output and income is recognized, the real source of economic progress is clarified. We improve our standard of living (income) by figuring out how to produce more output (things that people value). Economic progress is dependent, for example, on our ability to build a better house, computer, or video camera with the same or a lesser amount of labor and other resources. Without increases in real output—that is, output adjusted for inflation—there can be no increases in income and improvement in our living standards.

Historical comparisons illustrate this point. On average, workers in North America, Europe, and Japan produce about five times more output per capita (per person) than their ancestors did 50 years ago. Similarly, their inflation-adjusted per capita income—what economists call real income—is approximately five times higher.

Output per worker also accounts for differences in earnings per worker across countries. For example, the average worker in the United States is better educated, works with more productive machines, and benefits from more efficient economic organization than the average person in India or China. Thus, the average U.S. worker produces approximately 20 times as much value of output as an average worker in India or China. American workers earn more because they produce more. If they did not produce more, they would not be able to earn more.

Politicians often erroneously talk as if the creation of jobs is the source of economic progress. While campaigning, former President Bush argued that his economic program had three pillars: "Jobs, jobs, and jobs." President Clinton stated that jobs were the centerpiece of his economic policy. Focusing on jobs is a potential source of confusion. More employment will not promote economic progress, unless the employment expands output. We do not need more jobs, per se. Rather we need more productive workers, more productivity-enhancing machinery, and more efficient economic organization so we can produce more output per capita.

Some observers argue that technology adversely affects workers. In fact, just the opposite is true. Once you recognize that expansion in output is the source of higher wages, the positive impact of improvements in technology is apparent: better technology makes it possible for workers to produce more and thus to earn more. For example, farmers can generally produce more when working with a tractor rather than a team of horses. Accountants can handle more business accounts using

14

micro-computers rather than a pencil and calculator. A secretary can prepare more letters when working with a word-processor rather than a typewriter.

Sometimes specific jobs will be eliminated. Clearly modern technology has largely eliminated the jobs of elevator operators, blacksmiths, household workers, ditch diggers, and buggy manufacturers. These changes, however, merely release human resources so they can be used to expand output in other areas. Other tasks can now be accomplished with the newly released resources and, as a result, we are able to achieve a higher standard of living than would otherwise be the case.

Recognition of the link between output and income also makes it easier to see why minimum wage legislation and labor unions fail to increase the overall wages of workers. A higher minimum wage will price some low-skill workers out of the market. Therefore, their employment will decline, reducing total output. While some individual workers may be helped, overall per capita income will be lower because per capita output will be lower.

Similarly, labor unions may be able to reduce the competition from nonunion workers and thereby push up the wages of union members. But without commensurate increases in worker productivity, unions are unable to enhance the wages of all workers. If they could, the average wages in a highly unionized country like the United Kingdom would be higher than in the United States. But this is not what we observe. Wages in the U.K. are at least 40 percent lower than in the U.S., even though nearly half of the workforce is unionized in the United Kingdom compared to less than 20 percent in the United States.

Without high productivity per worker, there can be no high wages per worker. Similarly, without growth in the production of goods and services valued by consumers, there can be no growth in the real income of a nation. Production provides the source of income.

Unless people produce more, they cannot earn more. Production of things people value is the source of income. Machinery and improvements in technology enhance both worker productivity and earnings.

6. The Four Sources of Income Growth are (a) Improvements in Worker Skills, (b) Capital Formation, (c) Technological Advancement, and (d) Better Economic Organization.

The goods and services that provide for our standard of living do not just happen. Their production requires work, investment, cooperation, machinery, brain power, and organization. There are four major sources of production and income growth.

First, improvements in the skills of workers will promote economic growth. Skillful workers are more productive. How do individuals improve their skills? Primarily they do so by investing in themselves—by developing their natural abilities. There are literally thousands of ways people can improve their skills, but most of them involve studying and practicing. Thus, education, training, and experience are the primary ways people improve their skills.

Second, capital formation can also enhance the productivity of workers. Workers can produce more if they work with more and better machines. For example, a logger can produce more when working with a chain saw rather than a hand-operated, cross-cut blade. Similarly, a transport worker can haul more with a truck than with a mule and wagon. Other things constant, investment in tools and machines can help us produce more in the future. But investment is not a free lunch. The resources used to produce tools, machines, and factories could also be used to produce food, clothing, automobiles, and other current consumption goods. Economics is about trade-offs. It does, however, indicate that people who save and invest more will be able to produce more in the future.

Third, an improvement in technology—our knowledge about how to transform resources into goods and services— will also permit us to achieve a larger future output. The use of brain power to discover economical new products and/or less costly methods of production is a powerful source of economic progress. During the last 250 years, improvements in technology have literally transformed our lives. During that time period, the steam engine and later the internal combustion engine, electricity, and nuclear power replaced human and animal power as the major source of energy. Automobiles, buses, trains, and airplanes replaced the horse and buggy (and walking) as the major methods of transportation. Technological improvements continue to change our lifestyles. Consider the impact of compact disk players, micro-computers, word-processors, microwave ovens, video cameras and cassette players, and automobile air conditioners—the development and improvement of these products during the last couple of decades have vastly changed the way that we work, play, and entertain ourselves.

Finally, improvements in economic organization can also promote economic growth. Of the four sources of growth, this one is probably the most often overlooked. The legal system of a country influences the degree of economic cooperation. Historically, legal innovations have been an important source of economic progress. During the 18th century, a system of patents provided investors with a private property right to their ideas. About the same time, the recognition of the corporation as a legal entity reduced the cost of forming large firms that were often required for the mass production of manufactured goods. Both of these improvements in economic organization accelerated the growth of output in Europe and North America.

Effective economic organization will facilitate social cooperation and channel resources toward the production of goods that people value. Conversely, economic organization that protects wasteful practices and fails to reward the creation of wealth will retard economic progress. In Part II we will investigate more fully the broad characteristics of effective economic organization.

7. Income is Compensation Derived from the Provision of Services to Others. People Earn Income by Helping Others.

People differ with regard to their productive abilities, preferences, opportunities, development of specialized skills, willingness to take risks, and luck. These differences influence incomes because they influence the value of the goods and services individuals will be able or willing to provide to others.

While considering differences among people, we must not lose sight of precisely what income is. Income is simply compensation received in exchange for productive services supplied to others. People who earn large incomes provide others with lots of things that they value. If they did not, other people would not be willing to pay them so generously. There is a moral here. If you want to earn a large income, you had better figure out how to help others a great deal. The converse is also true. If you are unable and unwilling to help others very much, your income will be quite small.

This direct link between helping others and receiving income provides each of us with a strong incentive to acquire skills and develop talents that are highly valued by others. College students study for long hours, endure stress, and incur the financial cost of schooling in order to become, for example, doctors, chemists, and engineers. Other people acquire training and experience that will help them develop electrician, maintenance, or computer programming skills. Still others invest and start a business. Why do people do these things? Many factors undoubtedly influence such decisions. In some cases, individuals may be motivated by a strong personal desire to improve the world in which we live. However, *and this is the key point*, even people who are motivated primarily by the pursuit of income will have a strong incentive to develop skills and undertake investments that are valuable to others. Provision of services that others value is the source of high earnings. Therefore, when markets determine incomes, even individuals motivated primarily by the pursuit of personal income will have a strong incentive to pay close attention to what it is that others value.

Some people have a tendency to think that high-income individuals must be exploiting others. Recognition that income is compensation received for helping others makes it easy to see the fallacy of this view. People who earn a large income almost always improve the well-being of large numbers of people. The entertainers and athletes who earn huge incomes do so because millions of people are willing to pay to see them perform. Business entrepreneurs who succeed in a big way do so by making their products affordable to millions of consumers. The late Sam Walton (founder of Walmart Stores) became the richest man in the United States because he figured out how to manage large inventories more effectively and bring discount prices on brand-name merchandise to small town America. Later, Bill Gates, the founder and president of Microsoft, rose to the top of the *Forbes* magazine "Wealthiest Four Hundred" list by developing a product that dramatically improved the efficiency and compatibility of desk-top computers. Millions of consumers who never heard of either Walton or Gates, nonetheless benefitted from their entrepreneurial talents and low-priced products. Walton and Gates made a lot of money because they helped a lot of people.

8. Profits Direct Businesses Toward Activities that Increase Wealth.

The people of a nation will be better off if their resources are used to produce goods and services that are highly valued in comparison with their costs. At any given time, there is virtually an infinite number of potential investment projects. Some will increase the value of resources and promote economic progress. Others will reduce the value of resources and lead to economic decline. If economic progress is going to proceed, the value-increasing projects must be encouraged and the value-reducing projects avoided.

This is precisely what profits and losses do in a market setting. Business firms purchase resources and use them to produce a product or service that is sold to consumers. Costs are incurred as the business pays workers and other resource owners for their services. If the sales of the business firm exceed the costs of employing all of the resources required to produce the firm's output, then the firm will make a profit. In essence, profit is a reward that business owners will earn if they produce a good that consumers value more (as measured by their willingness to pay) than the resources required for the good's production (as measured by the cost of bidding the resources away from their alternative employment possibilities).

In contrast, losses are a penalty imposed on businesses that reduce the value of resources. The value of the resources used up by such unsuccessful firms exceeds the price consumers are willing to pay for their product. Losses and bankruptcies are the market's way of bringing such wasteful activities to a halt.

For example, suppose that it costs a shirt manufacturer $20,000 per month to lease a building, rent the required

If a nation is going to get the most out of its resources, it must have a way of bringing counterproductive activities to a halt. In market economies, losses perform this vitally important function.

machines, and purchase the labor, cloth, buttons, and other materials necessary to produce and market 1,000 shirts per month. If the manufacturer sells the 1,000 shirts for $22 each, his actions create wealth. Consumers value the shirts more than they value the resources required for their production. The manufacturer's $2 profit per shirt is a reward received for increasing the value of the resources.

On the other hand, if the shirts could not be sold for more than $17 each, then the manufacturer would show a loss of $3 per shirt. This loss results because the manufacturer's actions reduced the value of the resources—the shirts were worth less to consumers than the resources required for their production.

We live in a world of changing tastes and technology, imperfect knowledge, and uncertainty. Business decision-makers cannot be sure of either future market prices or costs of production. Their decisions must be based on expectations. Nonetheless, the reward-penalty structure of a market economy is clear. Firms that produce efficiently and anticipate correctly the products and services for which future demand will be most urgent (relative to production cost) will make economic profits. Those that are inefficient and allocate resources incorrectly into areas of weak future demand will be penalized with losses.

Essentially, profits and losses direct business investment toward projects that promote economic progress and away from those that squander scarce resources. This is a vitally important function. Nations that fail to perform this function well will almost surely experience economic stagnation.

9. The "Invisible Hand" Principle—Market Prices Bring Personal Self-interest and the General Welfare into Harmony.

Every individual is continually exerting himself to find out the most advantageous employment for whatever capital he can command. It is his own advantage, indeed, and not that of the society which he has in view. But the study of his own advantage naturally, or rather necessarily, leads him to prefer that employment which is most advantageous to society.... He intends only his own gain, and he is in this, and in many other cases, led by an invisible hand to promote an end which was not part of his intention.[1]

—**Adam Smith**

As Adam Smith noted, the remarkable thing about an economy based on private property and freedom of contract is that market prices will bring the actions of self-interested individuals into harmony with the general prosperity of a community or nation. The entrepreneur "intends only his own gain" but he is directed by the "invisible hand" of market prices to "promote an end [economic prosperity] which was not part of his intention."

The invisible hand principle is difficult for many people to grasp because there is a natural tendency to associate order with centralized planning. If resources are going to be allocated sensibly, surely some central authority must be in charge. The invisible hand principle stresses that this need not be the case. When private property and freedom of exchange are present, market prices will register the choices of literally millions of consumers, producers, and resource suppliers and bring them into harmony. Prices will reflect information about consumer preferences, costs, and matters related to timing, location, and circumstances

Price controls cause shortages. For example, when price controls were imposed on gasoline, they led to long waiting lines and "no gas" signs at the pump. This was true for both the U.S. during the 1970s and Eastern Europe during the 1990s.

that are well beyond the comprehension of any individual or central-planning authority. This single summary statistic—the market price—provides producers with everything they need to know in order to bring their actions into harmony with the actions and preferences of others. The market price directs and motivates both producers and resource suppliers to provide those things that others value highly, relative to their costs.

No central authority is needed to tell business decision-makers what to produce or how to produce it. Prices will do the job. For example, no one has to force the farmer to raise wheat, or tell the construction firm to build houses, or convince the furniture manufacturer to produce chairs. When the prices of these and other products indicate that consumers value them as much or more than their production costs, producers seeking personal gain will supply them.

Neither will it be necessary or even helpful for a central authority to monitor the production methods of business firms. Farmers, construction companies, furniture manufacturers, and thousand of other producers will seek out the best resource combination and most cost-effective production methods because lower costs mean higher profits. It is in the interest of each producer to keep costs down and quality up. In fact, competition virtually forces them to do so. High-cost producers will have difficulty surviving in the marketplace. Consumers, seeking the best value for their money, will see to that.

The invisible hand of the market process works so automatically that most people give little thought to it. Most simply take it for granted that goods people value will be produced in approximately the quantities that consumers want to buy them. The long waiting lines and "sold out until next week" signs that characterize centrally-planned economies are almost totally unknown to the residents of market economies. Similarly, the availability of a vast array of goods that challenges even the imagination of modern consumers is largely taken for granted. The invisible hand process brings order, harmony, and diversity. The process works so quietly, however, that it is both little understood and seldom appreciated. Nonetheless, it is vital to our economic well-being.

10. Ignoring Secondary Effects and Long-term Consequences is the Most Common Source of Error in Economics.

Henry Hazlitt, perhaps this century's greatest popular writer on economics, authored the book *Economics in One Lesson*. Hazlitt's one lesson was, that when analyzing an economic proposal, one:

> *must trace not merely the immediate results but the results in the long run, not merely the primary consequences but the secondary consequences, and not merely the effects on some special group but the effects on everyone.*[2]

Hazlitt believed that failure to apply this lesson was, by far, the most common source of economic error.

It is difficult to argue with this point. Time and again, politicians stress the short-term benefits derived from a policy, while completely ignoring longer-term consequences. Similarly, there seems to be an endless pleading for proposals to help specific industries, regions, or groups without considering their impact on the broader community, including taxpayers and consumers.

Of course, much of this is deliberate. When seeking political favors, interest groups and their hired representatives have an incentive to put the best spin on their case. Predictably, they will exaggerate the benefits, while ignoring important components of costs. When the benefits are immediate and easily visible, while the costs are less visible and mostly in the future, it will be easier for interest groups to sell befuddled economic reasoning.

It is easy to point to instances where the secondary effects are largely ignored. Consider the case of rent controls imposed on apartments. Proponents argue that controls will reduce rents and make housing more affordable for the poor. Yes, but there will be secondary effects. The lower rental prices will depress the rate of return on housing investments. Current owners of rental units may be forced to accept the lower return, but this will not be true for potential future owners. Many of them will channel their funds elsewhere; apartment house investments will fall; and the future availability of rental units will decline. Shortages will develop and the quality of rental housing will fall with the passage of time. These secondary effects, however, will not be immediately observable. Thus, rent controls command substantial popularity in communities ranging from New York City to Berkeley, California, even though a declining supply of rental housing, poor maintenance, and shortages are the inevitable results. In the words of Swedish economist Assar Lindbeck: "In many cases rent control appears to be the most efficient technique presently known to destroy a city—except for bombing."[3]

The proponents of tariffs and quotas to "protect jobs" almost always ignore the secondary effects of their policies. Consider the impact of trade restrictions that reduce the supply of foreign-produced automobiles in the U.S. market. As a result, employment in the domestic automobile industry expands. But what about the secondary effects on others? The restrictions will mean higher prices for automobile consumers. As a result of the higher prices, many auto consumers will be forced to curtail their purchases of food, clothing, recreation, and literally thousands of other items. These reductions in spending will mean less output and reduced employment in these areas. Furthermore, there is also a secondary effect on foreigners. Since foreigners sell fewer automobiles to Americans, they acquire fewer dollars with which to import American-made goods. When foreigners sell less to us, they will have less purchasing power with which to buy from us. Therefore, U.S. exports will fall as a result of the restrictions on automobile imports. Once the secondary effects are considered, the impact on employment is clear. The restrictions do not create jobs; they reshuffle them. Employment is higher in the auto industry, but lower in other industries, particularly export industries. Unfortunately, the jobs of the people actual working in the automobile industry are highly visible, while the secondary effects— the "lost jobs" in other industries—are less visible. Thus, it is not surprising that many people fall for the "protecting jobs" argument even though it is clearly fallacious.

Let's consider one final misconception that reflects a failure to consider the secondary effects. Politicians often argue that government spending on favored projects expands employment. Of course, there may be good reasons for government expenditures on roads, increased police protection, administration of justice, and so forth. The creation of jobs, however, is not one of them. Suppose the government spends $50 billion employing one million workers to build a high speed train linking Los Angeles and San Diego. How many jobs will the project create? Once the secondary effects are considered, the answer is none. The government must either use taxes or debt to finance the project. Taxes of $50 billion will reduce both consumer spending and private savings and thereby destroy as many jobs as the government spending will create. Alternatively, if the project is financed by debt, the borrowing will lead to higher interest rates and a decline in $50 billion of private investment and consumption expenditures. As in the case of trade restrictions, the result is job re-shufflement, not job creation. Does this mean the project should not be undertaken? Not necessarily. But it does mean that its justification must come from benefits provided by the high-speed train rather than the illusory benefits of an expansion in employment.

PART II:

Seven Major Sources of

Economic Progress

SEVEN MAJOR SOURCES OF ECONOMIC PROGRESS

1. Private Ownership: People Will Be More Industrious and Use Resources More Wisely When Property is Privately Owned.

2. Freedom of Exchange: Policies that Reduce the Volume of Exchange Retard Economic Progress.

3. Competitive Markets: Competition Promotes the Efficient Use of Resources and Provides a Continuous Stimulus for Innovative Improvements.

4. An Efficient Capital Market: If a Nation is Going to Realize its Potential, It Must Have a Mechanism Capable of Allocating Capital Toward Wealth-Creating Projects.

5. Monetary Stability: Inflationary Monetary Policies Distort Price Signals and Undermine a Market Economy.

6. Low Tax Rates: People Will Produce More When They are Permitted to Keep More of What They Earn.

7. Free Trade: A Nation Can Gain by Selling Goods that It Can Produce at a Relatively Low Cost and Using the Proceeds to Buy Things that It Can Produce Only at a High Cost.

1. Private Ownership: People Will Be More Industrious and Use Resources More Wisely When Property is Privately Owned.

Men always work harder and more readily when they work on that which belongs to them....It is surely undeniable that, when a man engages in remunerative work, the impelling reason and motive of his work is to obtain property and thereafter to hold it as his very own.

—Pope Leo XIII (1878)

Private ownership of property involves three things: (a) the right to exclusive use, (b) legal protection against invaders, and (c) the right to transfer. Property is a broad term that includes labor services, ideas, literature, and natural resources, as well as physical assets like buildings, machines, and land. Private ownership allows individuals to decide how they will use their property. But it also makes them accountable for their actions. People who use their property in a manner that invades or infringes upon the property rights of another will be subject to the same legal forces that were set up to protect their own property. For example, private property rights prohibit me from throwing my hammer through the screen of a computer that you own, because if I did, I would be violating your property right to your computer. Your property right to your computer restricts me and everyone else from its use without your permission. Similarly, my ownership of my hammer and other things that I own restricts you and everyone else from using them without my permission.

The important thing about private ownership is the structure of incentives that emanate from it. There are four major reasons why this incentive structure will promote economic progress.

First, private ownership encourages wise stewardship. If private owners fail to maintain their property or if they allow it to be abused or damaged, they will bear the consequences in the form of a decline in the value of their property. For example, if you own an automobile, you have a strong incentive to change the oil, have the car serviced regularly, and see that the interior of the car is well kept. Why is this so? If you are careless in these areas, the car's value to both you and potential future owners will decline. Alternatively, if the car is well-maintained and kept in good running order, it will be of greater value to both you and others who might want to buy it from you. With private ownership, wise stewardship is rewarded.

In contrast, when property is owned by the government or owned in common by a large group of people, the incentive to take good care of it is weaker. For example when housing is owned by the government, there is no owner or small group of owners who will pay a dear price if the property is abused and poorly maintained. Therefore, it should not surprise us when we observe that, compared to privately-owned housing, government-owned housing is generally run down and poorly maintained in both capitalist counties like the United States and socialist counties like Russia and Poland. This laxity in care, maintenance, and repair simply reflects the incentive structure that accompanies government ownership of property.

Second, private ownership encourages people to develop their property and use it productively. With private ownership, individuals have a strong incentive to improve their skills, work harder, and work smarter. Such actions will increase their income. Similarly, people have a strong incentive to construct and develop capital assets like houses, apartments, and office buildings. When such developments add more to revenues than to costs, the wealth of the private owners will increase.

Farming in the former Soviet Union illustrates the importance of property rights as a stimulus for productive activity. Under the Communist regime, families were permitted to keep and/or sell all goods produced on small private plots ranging up to an acre in size. These private plots made up only one percent of the total land under cultivation; the other 99 percent was cultivated by state enterprises and huge agricultural cooperatives. Nonetheless, as the Soviet press reported, approximately one-fourth of the total Soviet agricultural output was raised on this tiny fraction of privately farmed land.

Third, private owners have a strong incentive to use their resources in ways that are beneficial to others. While private owners can legally "do their own thing" with their property, their ownership provides them with a strong incentive to heed the wishes of *others*. Private owners can gain by figuring out how to make their property and its services more attractive *to others*. If they employ and develop their property in ways that *others* find attractive, the market value of the property will increase. In contrast, changes that are disapproved of by others—particularly customers or potential future buyers—will reduce the value of one's property.

Your ownership of your labor services provides you with a strong incentive to invest in education and training that will help you provide services that are highly valued *by others*. Similarly, owners of capital assets have an incentive to develop them in ways that are attractive *to others*. By way of example, consider the situation of an apartment complex owner. The owner may not care anything about parking spaces, convenient laundry facilities, trees, or well kept "green" open spaces accompanying the apartment complex. However, if consumers value these things highly (relative to their costs), the owner has a strong incentive to provide them because they will enhance both his earnings (rents) and the market value of his apartments. In contrast, those apartment owners who insist on providing what they like, rather than the things that consumers actually prefer, will find that their earnings and the value of their capital (apartments) will decline.

Fourth, private ownership promotes the wise development and conservation of resources for the future. The present development of a resource may generate current revenue. This revenue is the voice of *present* consumers. But, higher potential future revenues argue for conservation. The potential gain in the form of an increase in the expected future price of the resource is the voice of *future* users. Private owners are encouraged to balance these two forces.

Whenever the expected future value of a resource exceeds its current value, private owners gain if they conserve the resource for future users. This is true even if the current owner does not expect to be around when the benefits accrue. For example, suppose a 65 year-old tree farmer is contemplating whether to cut his Douglas fir trees. If growth and increased scarcity are expected to result in future sales revenue that exceeds the current value of the trees, the farmer will gain by conserving the trees for the future. When ownership is transferable, the market value of the farmer's land will increase in anticipation of the future harvest as the trees grow and the expected day of harvest moves closer. Thus, the farmer will be able to sell the trees (or the land including the trees) and capture their value at any time even though the actual harvest may not take place until well after his death.[4]

For centuries, doomsday commentators have argued that we are about to run out of trees, vital minerals, or various sources of energy. In sixteenth-century England, fear arose that the supply of wood would soon be exhausted as that resource was widely used as a source of energy. Higher wood prices, however, encouraged conservation and led to the development of coal. The "wood crisis" soon dissipated. In the middle of the nineteenth century, dire predictions arose that the United States was about to run out of whale oil, at the time the primary fuel for artificial lighting. As whale oil prices rose, pressures for a substitute energy source heightened. This led to the development of kerosene and the end of the "whale oil crisis."

Later, as people switched to petroleum, doomsday predictions about the exhaustion of this resource arose almost as soon as the resource was developed. In 1914, the Bureau of Mines reported that the total U.S. supply of oil was 6 million barrels, an amount less than the U.S. now produces approximately every 20 months. In 1926, the Federal Oil Conservation Board informed people that the U.S. supply of oil would last only seven years. A couple of decades later the Secretary of Interior forecast that the U.S. would run out of oil in just a few more years. A study sponsored by the Club of Rome made similar predictions for the world during the 1970s. Of course, time has proven all of these forecasts wrong.

Doomsday forecasters fail to recognize that private ownership provides people with a strong incentive to conserve a valuable resource and search for substitutes when there is an increase in the relative scarcity of the resource. With private ownership, if the scarcity of a resource increases, the price of the resource will rise. The increase in price provides producers, innovators, engineers, and entrepreneurs with an incentive to (a) conserve on the direct use of the resource, (b) search more diligently for substitutes, and (c) develop new methods of discovering and recovering larger amounts of the resource. To date, these forces have pushed doomsday further and further into the future. For resources that are privately owned, there is every reason to believe that they will continue to do so.[5]

People who have not thought the topic through often associate private ownership with selfishness. This is paradoxical since the truth is nearly the opposite. Private ownership both (a) provides protection against selfish people who would take what does not belong to them and (b) forces resource users to fully bear the cost of their actions. When property rights are well-defined, secure, and tradeable, suppliers of goods and services will have to provide resource owners with at least as good a deal as they can get elsewhere. Employers cannot seize and use scarce resources without compensating their owners. The resource owners will have to be paid enough to attract them away from alternative users.

In essence, securely defined private property rights eliminate the use of violence as a competitive weapon. A producer that you do not buy from is not permitted to burn down your house. Neither is a competitive resource supplier, whose prices you undercut, permitted to slash your automobile tires or threaten you with bodily injury.

Private ownership keeps power dispersed and expands the area of activity that is based on voluntary consent. Power conferred by private ownership is strictly limited. Private business owners cannot force you to buy from them or work for them. They cannot levy a tax on your income or your property. They can acquire some of your income only by giving you something that you believe to be more valuable in return. The power of even the wealthiest property owner (or largest business) is limited by competition from others willing to provide similar products or services.

In contrast, as the experience of Eastern Europe and the former Soviet Union illustrates, when government ownership is substituted for private property, enormous political and economic power is bestowed upon a small handful of political figures. One of the major virtues of private property is its ability to check the excessive concentration of economic power in the hands of the few. Widespread ownership of property is the enemy of tyranny and the abusive use of power.

Thus, it is clear what the former socialist countries need to do. As Nobel laureate Milton Friedman recently stated, the best program for Eastern Europe can be summarized "in three words: privatize, privatize, privatize."[6] Private property is the cornerstone of both economic progress and personal liberty.

2. Freedom of Exchange: Policies that Reduce the Volume of Exchange Retard Economic Progress.

Voluntary exchange is a form of social cooperation. It permits both parties to get more of what they want. In a market setting, neither the buyer nor the seller is forced into an exchange. Personal gain provides the motivation for exchange agreements.

As we previously noted, exchange promotes social gain—a larger output and income than would otherwise be achievable. When governments impose blockades that limit cooperation through exchange, they stifle economic progress.

There are various ways that countries stifle exchange. *First, many countries impose regulations that limit entry into various businesses and occupations.* If you want to start a business or provide a service, you have to fill out forms, get permission from different bureaus, show that you are qualified, indicate that you have sufficient financing, and meet various other regulatory tests. Some officials may refuse your application unless you are willing to pay a bribe or make a contribution to their political coffers. Hernando De Soto, in his revealing book *The Other Path*, found that in Lima, Peru it took 289 days for five people working full-time to meet the regulations required to legally open a small business producing garments. Furthermore, along the way, ten bribes were solicited and on two occasions it was necessary to pay the bribes in order to get the permission to operate "legally." In many cases, if you are financed with foreign capital there is an additional maze of regulations. Needless to say, policies of this type stifle business competition, encourage political corruption, and drive decent people into the underground (or what De Soto calls the "informal") economy.

Second, countries also stifle exchange when they substitute discretionary political authority for the rule of law. Several countries make a habit of adopting high-sounding laws that grant political administrators substantial interpretive power and discretionary authority. For example, in the mid-1980s customs officials in Guatemala were permitted to waive tariffs if they thought that doing so was in the "national interest." Legislation of this type is an open invitation for government officials to solicit bribes. It creates regulatory uncertainty and makes business activity more costly and less attractive, particularly for honest people. The structure of law needs to be precise, unambiguous, and nondiscriminatory. If it is not, it will be a major roadblock retarding gains from trade.

Third, many countries impose price controls that stifle exchange. When the price of a product is legally fixed above the market level, buyers will purchase fewer units and the quantity exchanged will fall. On the other hand, if the price is fixed lower than the market level, suppliers will be unwilling to produce as many units. This, too, will reduce the volume of exchange. In terms of units produced and sold, it makes little difference whether price controls push prices up or force them down; both will reduce the volume of trade and the gains from production and exchange.

Exchange is productive; it helps us get more from the available resources. Policies that force traders to pass through various political roadblocks are generally counterproductive, even when they are intended to protect a domestic industry. In fact, they are equivalent to shooting oneself in the foot. If a country is going to realize its full potential, restrictions limiting trade and increasing the cost of doing business need to be kept to a minimum. The ability to provide a service that others are willing to purchase voluntarily is powerful evidence that the activity is productive. The market is the best regulator.

3. Competitive Markets: Competition Promotes the Efficient Use of Resources and Provides a Continuous Stimulus for Innovative Improvements.

Competition is conducive to the continuous improvements of industrial efficiency. It leads...producers to eliminate wastes and cut costs so that they may undersell others.... It weeds out those whose costs remain high and thus operates to concentrate production in the hands of those whose costs are low.[7]

—Clair Wilcox

Competition occurs when there is freedom of entry into a market and alternative sellers in the market. The competition may be among small-scale or large-scale firms. Rival firms may compete in local, regional, national, or even global markets. Competition is the lifeblood of a market economy.

Competition places pressure on producers to operate efficiently and cater to the preferences of consumers. Competition weeds out the inefficient. Firms that fail to provide consumers with quality goods at competitive prices will experience losses and eventually be driven out of business. Successful competitors have to outperform rival firms. They may do so through a variety of methods—quality of product, style, service, convenience of location, advertising, and price—but they must consistently offer consumers as much or more value than they can get elsewhere.

What keeps McDonald's, General Motors, or any other business firm from raising prices, selling shoddy products, and providing lousy service? Competition provides the answer. If McDonald's fails to provide an attractively priced sandwich with a smile, people will turn to Burger King, Wendy's, Dairy Queen, and other rivals. Similarly, as recent experience has shown, even a firm as large as General Motors will lose customers to Ford, Honda, Toyota, Chrysler, Volkswagen, Mazda, and other automobile manufacturers if it fails to keep up with its rivals.

Competition also provides firms with a strong incentive to develop improved products and discover lower-cost methods of production. No one knows precisely what products consumers will want next or which production techniques will minimize per-unit costs. Competition helps us discover the answer. Is that new visionary idea the greatest thing since the development of the fast-food chain? Or is it simply another dream that will soon turn to vapor? Entrepreneurs are free to introduce that innovative new product or promising production technology; they need only the support of investors willing to put up the necessary funds. The approval of central planners, a legislative majority, or business rivals is not required in a market economy. Nonetheless, competition holds entrepreneurs and the investors who support them accountable; their ideas must face a "reality check" imposed by consumers. If consumers value the innovative idea enough to cover the cost of the good or service that is produced, the new business will prosper and succeed. Conversely, if consumers are unwilling to do so, the business will fail. Consumers are the ultimate judge and jury of business innovation and performance.

Producers who wish to survive in a competitive environment cannot be complacent. Today's successful product may not pass tomorrow's competitive test. In order to succeed in a competitive market, businesses must be good at anticipating, identifying, and quickly adopting improved ideas.

Competition is the disciplining force of a market economy. The presence of alternative sellers more or less forces business firms to cater to the wishes of consumers and search for better ways of doing things.

Competition also discovers the type of business structure and size of firm that can best keep the per-unit cost of a product or service low. Unlike other economic systems, a market economy does not mandate or limit the types of firms that are permitted to compete. Any form of business organization is permissible. An owner-operated firm, partnership, corporation, employee-owned firm, consumer cooperative, commune, or any other form of business is free to enter the market. In order to be successful, it has to pass only one test: cost-effectiveness. If a form of business organization, such as a corporation or employee-owned firm, is able to achieve low per-unit cost in a market, it will tend to survive. Correspondingly, a business structure that results in high per-unit cost will be driven from a competitive market.

The same is true for size of firm. For some products, a business must be quite large to take full advantage of the potential production economies of scale. When per-unit costs decline as output increases, small businesses tend to have higher production costs (and therefore higher prices) than their larger counterparts. When this is the case, consumers interested in maximum value for their money will tend to buy from the lower-priced larger firm. Most small firms will eventually be driven from the market. Larger firms, generally organized as corporations, tend to survive in such markets. The auto and airplane manufacturing industries illustrate these forces.

In other instances, small firms, often organized as individual proprietorships or partnerships, will be more cost-effective. When personalized service and individualized products are valued highly by consumers, it may be difficult for large firms to compete. Under these circumstances, mostly small firms will survive. For example, this is generally true for law and medical practices, printing shops, and hair-styling salons. A market economy permits cost considerations and the interaction between producers and consumers to determine the type and size of firm in each market.

When large-scale enterprises have lower costs, it will be particularly important that nations do not either limit competition from foreign suppliers or prevent domestic firms from selling abroad. This point is vitally important for small countries. For example, since the domestic market of a country like South Korea is small, a Korean automobile manufacturer would have extremely high costs per unit if it could not sell automobiles abroad. Similarly, domestic consumers in small countries would have to pay an exceedingly high price for automobiles if they were prohibited from buying from large-scale, lower-cost foreign producers.

When harnessed by competition, self-interest provides business with a strong incentive to serve the interests of consumers.

In summary, competition harnesses personal self-interest and puts it to work elevating our standard-of-living. As Adam Smith noted in the *Wealth of Nations*, individuals are motivated by self-interest:

> *It is not from the benevolence of the butcher, the brewer, or the baker, that we expect our dinner, but from their regard to their own self-interest. We address ourselves not to their humanity but to their self-love, and never talk to them of our own necessities, but of their advantages.*[8]

In a competitive environment, even self-interested individuals and profit-seeking business firms have a strong incentive to serve the interests of others and provide consumers with at least as much value as they can get elsewhere. This is the path to greater income and larger profits. Paradoxical as it may seem, personal self-interest—a characteristic many view as less than admirable—is a powerful source of economic progress when it is directed by competition.

4. An Efficient Capital Market: If a Nation is Going to Realize Its Potential, It Must Have a Mechanism Capable of Allocating Capital into Wealth-Creating Projects.

Consumption is the goal of all production. However, we can sometimes magnify our production of consumption goods by first using resources to produce machines, heavy equipment, and buildings and then applying these capital resources to the production of the desired consumer goods. Therefore, investment—the construction and development of long-lasting resources designed to help us produce more in the future—is an important potential source of economic growth.

Resources used to produce investment goods will be unavailable for the direct production of consumption goods. Therefore, investment requires savings—the forgoing of current consumption. Someone—either the investor or someone willing to supply funds to the investor—must save in order to finance investment. Funds cannot be invested unless they are saved.

Not all investment projects will create wealth. If an investment project is going to enhance the wealth of a nation, the value of the *additional* output derived from the investment must exceed the cost of the investment. Conversely, when the value of the additional output is less than the cost of the investment, the project is counterproductive. Projects of this type reduce wealth. If a nation is going to realize its potential, it must have a mechanism capable of attracting savings and channelling them into wealth-creating investment projects.

In a market economy, the capital market performs this function. This highly diverse market includes the markets for stocks, real estate, and businesses, as well as the loanable funds market. Financial institutions such as banks, insurance companies, mutual funds, and investment firms play important roles in this market. The capital market coordinates the actions of savers who supply funds to the market and investors seeking funds to finance various business activities. Private investors have a strong incentive to evaluate potential projects carefully and search for profitable projects. Investors ranging from stockholders to partnership investors to small business owners will search for and undertake profitable ventures because such investments will increase their personal wealth. Profitable investments generally create wealth. A project will be profitable if the revenues derived from the additions to output exceed the cost of the investment. Revenues that exceed the costs of an investment are strong evidence that people value the output of the investment more than the resources required to produce the capital asset. Thus, profitable investments tend to increase not only the wealth of the investor, but also the wealth of the nation.

Of course, in an uncertain world, private investors will sometimes make mistakes; sometimes they undertake projects that prove to be unprofitable. If investors were unwilling to take such chances, many new ideas would go untested and many worthwhile, but risky, projects would not be undertaken. Mistaken investments are a necessary price paid for fruitful innovations in new technologies and products. Counterproductive projects, however, must be brought to a halt. The capital market assures that this will be the case. Private investors will not continue to waste their funds on unprofitable and unproductive projects.

Without a private capital market, it is virtually impossible to attract funds and consistently channel them into wealth-creating projects. When investment funds are allocated by the government rather than the market, an entirely different set of criteria come into play. Political clout replaces the expected return on investment as the

Exhibit 1: Capital Markets, Real Interest Rates, and the Growth of Per Capita GDP in Developing Countries

Countries with Negative Real Interest Rates	Real Interest Rate[a]		Annual Growth Rate of Per Capita GDP, 1980-1990
	1983-85	1988-90	
Argentina	-163	-1179	-1.7
Zambia	-16	-77	-2.8
Somalia	-35	-69	-0.7
Uganda	-74	-65	0.3
Sierra Leone	-37	-41	-0.9
Ecuador	-19	-21	-0.4
Ghana	-46	-15	-0.4
Tanzania	-21	-12	-0.3

[a] The real interest rate is equal to the nominal deposit interest rate during a year minus the inflation rate.

Source: World Bank, *World Development Report (annual)* and *World Tables: 1990-1992* edition.

basis for allocating funds. Investment funds will often be channeled to political supporters and to projects that benefit individuals and groups with political clout.

When politics replaces markets, investment projects often reduce wealth rather than enhance it. The experience of Eastern Europe and the former Soviet Union illustrates this point. For four decades (1950–90), the investment rates of these countries were among the highest in the world. Central planners allocated approximately one-third of the national output into investment. Even these high rates of investment, however, did little to improve living standards because political rather than economic considerations determined which projects would be funded. Resources were often wasted on political boondoggles and high visibility investments favored by important political leaders.

Sometimes governments fix interest rates and thereby hamper the ability of markets to channel personal savings toward wealth-creating projects. Worse still, when an interest rate ceiling is combined with inflationary monetary policy, the interest rate adjusted for inflation—what economists call the "real interest rate"—will often be negative! When the government-mandated interest rate is less than the rate of inflation, the wealth of people who save is reduced. Their savings and interest earnings will buy less and less with the passage of time. Under these circumstances, there will be little incentive to save and supply funds to the domestic capital market. "Capital flight" will result as domestic investors seek positive returns abroad and foreign investors completely shun the country. Such policies destroy the domestic capital market. Lacking both financial capital and a mechanism to direct investment toward wealth-creating projects, productive investment in such countries comes to a standstill. Income stagnates and even regresses.

As Exhibit 1 illustrates, Argentina, Zambia, Somalia, Uganda, Sierra Leone, Ecuador, Ghana and Tanzania followed this course during the 1980s. All of these countries fixed the interest rate and followed an inflationary monetary policy. As a result, the inflation-adjusted interest rate—the real return on savings deposits—was negative throughout much of the 1980s in each of these countries! So, too, was their growth rate.

These countries followed policies that destroyed the mechanism that would normally provide potential private investors with loanable funds and channel those funds toward wealth-creating projects. Lacking a mechanism to perform this vitally important function, they regressed during the 1980s. Countries that destroy their capital markets pay a severe price for their folly.

49

5. Monetary Stability: Inflationary Monetary Policies Distort Price Signals and Undermine a Market Economy.

First and foremost, money is a means of exchange. It reduces transaction costs because it provides a common denominator into which all goods and services can be converted. Money makes it possible for people to engage in complex exchanges involving the receipt of income or payment of a purchase price across lengthy time periods. Money provides us with a means through which we can store purchasing power for future use. Money is also a unit of accounting that enhances our ability to keep track of revenues and costs that are incurred across time periods.

The productive contribution of money, however, is directly related to the stability of its value. In this regard, money is to an economy what language is to communication. Without words that have clearly defined meanings to both the speaker and listener, communication is impossible. So it is with money. If money does not have a stable and predictable value, it will be more costly for borrowers and lenders to conduct exchanges; saving and investing will involve additional risks; and time-dimension transactions (for example, the payment of the purchase price for a house or automobile over a time period) will be fraught with additional danger. When the value of money is unstable, exchange is retarded and the gains from specialization, large-scale production, and social cooperation are reduced.

There is no mystery about the cause of monetary instability. Like other commodities, the value of money is determined by supply and demand. When the supply money is constant or increases at a slow steady rate, the purchasing power of money will be relatively stable. In contrast, when the supply of money expands rapidly and unpredictably relative to the supply of goods and services, prices are inflated and the purchasing power of money declines. This often happens when governments print money (or borrow from a central bank) in order to pay their bills.

Politicians often blame inflation on greedy businesses, powerful labor unions, big oil companies, or foreigners, for example. But their efforts are a ruse—a diversionary tactic. Both economic theory and historical experience indicate that persistent inflation arises from a single source: rapid growth in the supply of money. Exhibit 2 illustrates this point. Countries that increased their money supply at a slow rate experienced low rates of inflation during the 1980s. This was true for large countries like Germany, Japan, and the United States, as well as for small countries like Switzerland, Netherlands, Cote d'Ivoire, and Cameroon. As the growth of the money supply of a country increased, however, so too did the rate of inflation (see data for Portugal, Venezuela, Costa Rica, Turkey, Ghana, Zaire, and Mexico). Extremely high rates of monetary-growth led to hyperinflation. This point was illustrated vividly by the experience of Israel, Peru, Argentina, and Bolivia. A triple-digit annual growth rate in the money supply of these countries led to a triple-digit annual rate of inflation.

Every country in the world with a low inflation rate in recent decades has adopted a policy of slow monetary growth. Conversely, every country that has experienced rapid inflation has followed a course of rapid monetary expansion. This link between rapid monetary growth and inflation is one of the most consistent relationships in all of economics.

Inflation undermines economic prosperity. It makes the planning and undertaking of capital investment projects extremely hazardous. Unexpected changes in the inflation rate can quickly turn an otherwise profitable project into a personal economic disaster. Given the additional

51

Exhibit 2: Monetary Growth and Inflation, 1980-1990

	Annual Growth Rate of the Money Supply	Annual Rate of Inflation
SLOW GROWTH OF THE MONEY SUPPLY		
Netherlands	2.8	1.9
Germany	4.0	2.7
Cote d'Ivoire	4.1	2.7
Japan	4.9	1.5
United States	5.0	3.7
Switzerland	5.1	3.7
Cameroon	5.6	5.6
RAPID GROWTH OF THE MONEY SUPPLY		
Portugal	13.2	18.2
Venezuela	16.8	19.3
Costa Rica	22.6	23.5
Ghana	41.8	42.7
Turkey	46.8	43.2
Mexico	61.4	70.4
Zaire	67.3	60.9
HYPER-GROWTH OF THE MONEY SUPPLY		
İsrael	98.6	101.4
Peru	157.3	233.7
Argentina	368.9	395.1
Bolivia	444.1	318.4

Source: The World Bank, *World Development Report, 1992* (tables 2 and 13). The growth rate of the money supply is equal to the nominal growth of the money supply minus the growth of real GDP.

uncertainty that accompanies high rates of inflation, many decision-makers will simply forgo capital investments and other transactions involving long-term commitments. Because of this, mutually advantageous trades will be curtailed and the potential gains from these exchanges will be lost.

During 1988, Brazil increased the quantity of Cruzados by approximately 800 percent. Prices rose by a similar amount. Excessive monetary expansion is the cause of inflation.

When governments inflate, people will spend less time producing and more time trying to protect their wealth. Since failure to anticipate accurately the rate of inflation can have a substantial effect on one's wealth, individuals will divert scarce resources away from the production of goods and services and into the acquisition of information on the future rate of inflation. The ability of business decision-makers to forecast changes in prices becomes more valuable than their ability to manage and organize production. Speculative practices are encouraged as persons try to outwit each other with regard to the future direction of prices. Funds flow into speculative investments like gold, silver, and art objects rather than into productive investments like buildings, machines, and technological research. As resources move from productive to unproductive activities, economic progress is retarded.

But perhaps the most destructive impact of inflation is that it undermines the creditability and confidence of citizens in their government. At the most basic level, people expect government to protect their person and property from intruders who would take what does not belong to them. When government become an intruder—when it cheats citizens by "watering down" the value of their currency—how can people have any confidence that the government will protect their property against other intrusions, enforce contracts, or punish unethical and criminal behavior? When the government "waters down" its currency, it is in a weak position to punish, for example, an orange juice producer that dilutes juice sold to customers or a business that waters down its stock (issues additional stock without permission of current stockholders).

Certain general principles are vital to the establishment of a stable monetary regime. First, if a country has a central bank that conducts monetary policy, the bank must be (a) independent of the political authorities and (b) held accountable for the maintenance of price stability. The most independent central bank in the world is the German Bundesbank. The Bundesbank Act of 1957 states that the bank "shall be independent of instructions from the federal government." Furthermore, the Bundesbank is obligated to support the economic policies of the government "only insofar as this support does not undermine its assigned task of preserving monetary stability."

In contrast, the central banks of Latin American countries have been almost entirely beholden to political officials. Under these regimes, central banking authorities who are unwilling to fund budget deficits with printing press money are often fired and replaced by someone "more cooperative." Not surprisingly, the German Bundesbank has one of the best inflation records in the world, while the politicized central banks of Latin America are best known for their inflationary policies.

Central bank authorities can be held accountable in various ways. They can be required by law to maintain the inflation rate (or a general price index or the rate of monetary growth) within a narrow range. Failure to do so might result in the dismissal of the bank's governing board. Alternatively, the salaries of the board and funds for operation might be tied to their record of monetary and price stability.

Some countries like Hong Kong and Singapore, for example, have set up a currency board as a means of achieving monetary stability. The currency board establishes a fixed rate of exchange between the currency that it issues and the currency of the reserve assets that it maintains. Under this arrangement, the currency board is required to maintain 100 percent reserves in the form of reserve assets such as U.S. dollars (and bonds). In essence, the 100 percent reserve requirement and agreement to exchange its currency for the foreign currency at the fixed rate ties the domestic currency to the foreign currency. Therefore, the inflation rate in a currency board country will be about the same as for the country whose bonds and currency are held as reserves.

While there are various ways that monetary and price stability can be achieved, there can be little question about its importance as a source of economic prosperity. Without monetary stability, potential gains from capital formation and other exchanges involving time commitments will be eroded and the people of the country will fail to realize their full potential.

6. Low Tax Rates: People Will Produce More When They are Permitted to Keep More of What They Earn.

Taxes are paid in the sweat of every man who labors. If those taxes are excessive, they are reflected in idle factories, in tax-sold farms, and in hordes of hungry people tramping streets and seeking jobs in vain.

—**Franklin Roosevelt**
in Pittsburgh, Oct. 19, 1932

When high tax rates take a large share of income, the incentive to work and use resources productively is reduced. The marginal tax rate—the share of additional income that is taxed away—is particularly important. As marginal tax rates increase, the share of additional earnings that individuals are permitted to keep declines.

There are three reasons why high marginal tax rates will reduce output and income. First, *high tax rates discourage work effort and reduce the productive efficiency of labor*. When marginal tax rates soar to 55 percent or 60 percent, individuals get to keep less than half of what they earn. People who do not get to keep much of what they earn tend not to earn very much. Some (for example, someone with a working spouse) will drop out of the labor force. Others will simply work fewer hours. Still others will decide to take more lengthy vacations, forgo overtime opportunities, retire earlier, be more particular about accepting jobs when unemployed, or forget about pursuing that promising but risky business venture. In some cases, high tax rates even drive a nation's most productive citizens to countries where taxes are lower. These substitutions will reduce the available labor supply, causing output to decline.

High tax rates will also result in inefficient utilization of labor. Some individuals will substitute less-productive activities that are not taxed (for example, do-it-yourself projects) for work opportunities yielding taxable income. Waste and economic inefficiency result.

Second, *high tax rates will reduce both the level and efficiency of capital formation.* High tax rates repel foreign investment and cause domestic investors to search for investment projects abroad where taxes are lower. Therefore, capital formation—which provides the fuel for economic growth—is retarded. Domestic investors will also turn to projects that shelter current income from taxation and away from projects with a higher rate of return but fewer tax-avoidance benefits. Business ventures that are designed to show an accounting loss in order to shelter income from the tax collector will become more widespread. As the result of the tax-shelter benefits, people are often able to gain from projects that reduce the value of resources. Scarce capital is wasted and resources are channeled away from their most productive uses.

Third, *high marginal tax rates encourage individuals to substitute less-desired tax deductible goods for more-desired, nondeductible goods.* Here the inefficiency stems from the fact that individuals do not bear the full cost of tax deductible purchases. High marginal tax rates make tax deductible expenditures cheap for persons in high tax brackets. Since the personal cost, *but not the cost to society*, is cheap, taxpayers confronting high marginal tax rates will spend more money on pleasurable, tax-deductible items, such as plush offices, Hawaiian business conferences, and various fringe benefits (for example, a company luxury automobile, business entertainment, and a company retirement plan). Since such tax deductible purchases reduce their taxes, people will often buy such goods even though they do not value them as much as it costs to produce them. Waste and inefficiency are byproducts of this incentive structure.

Exhibit 3: Marginal Tax Rates and Economic Growth

	Top Marginal Rate		Annual Growth Rate of Per Capita GDP, 1980-1990
	1984	1989	
High Tax Countries			
Iran	90	75	−1.2
Morocco	87	87	1.4
Zambia	80	75[a]	−2.9
Dominican Republic	73	73	−0.1
Tanzania	95	50[a]	−0.3
Zimbabwe	63	60	−0.5
Zaire	60[a]	60[a]	−1.4
Cameroon	60	60	−0.7
Ghana	60[a]	55[a]	−0.4
Average Growth Rate			**−0.7**
Low Tax Countries			
Hong Kong	25	25	5.7
Indonesia	35	35	3.7
Mauritius	30	35	5.0
Singapore	40	33	4.2
Malaysia	45	45	2.6
Average Growth Rate			**4.2**

[a]   Indicates that the top rate applied at an equivalent income level of less than $10,000.

Source: The marginal tax rate data are from Price Waterhouse, *Individual Tax Rates, 1984 and 1989.* The growth rate data are from the World Bank, *World Development Report, 1992.*

In short, economic analysis indicates that high tax rates will reduce productive activity, retard capital formation, and promote wasteful use of resources. Predictably, the income of a country that imposes high marginal tax rates will fall below its potential.

As Exhibit 3 shows, several less-developed countries levy exceedingly high marginal tax rates and these rates are often applied at a very low income level. For example, in 1989 Tanzania levied a 50 percent tax on virtually all personal income. Thus, people got to keep only half of what they earned. Similarly, persons with equivalent incomes of less than $10,000 U.S. dollars confronted marginal tax rates of between 55 percent and 75 percent in Zambia, Ghana, and Zaire. Top marginal tax rates of 60 percent or more were levied in Iran, Morocco, Dominican Republic, Zimbabwe, and Cameroon. Not surprisingly, the average real per capita Gross Domestic Product (GDP) of these high tax countries actually declined during the 1980s. Only one of the high tax countries (Morocco) was able to achieve any growth during the decade.

In contrast, marginal tax rates were much lower in five less developed countries; Hong Kong, Indonesia, Mauritius, Singapore, and Malaysia. These low-tax countries enjoyed rapid economic growth. Their real per capita GDP grew at an annual rate of 4.2 percent during the 1980s. High tax rates are an obstacle to prosperity and the growth of income. Governments that want to promote prosperity will strive to keep tax rates, particularly marginal tax rates, low.

7. Free Trade: A Nation Can Gain by Selling Goods that It Can Produce at a Relatively Low Cost and Using the Proceeds to Buy Things that It Can Produce Only at a High Cost.

Free trade consists simply in letting people buy and sell as they want to buy and sell.... Protective tariffs are as much applications of force as are blockading squadrons, and their objective is the same—to prevent trade. The difference between the two is that blockading squadrons are a means whereby nations seek to prevent their enemies from trading; protective tariffs are a means whereby nations attempt to prevent their own people from trading.[9]

—Henry George (1886)

The principles involved in international trade are basically the same as those involved in any other voluntary exchange: the exchange enables each trading partner to produce and consume more than would otherwise be achievable. There are three reasons why this is so.

First, with international trade the people of each nation will be able to use more of their resources to produce and sell things that they do well and use the proceeds to purchase goods that they could produce only at a high cost. Resource endowments differ substantially across countries. These differences influence costs. Goods that are quite costly to produce in one country may be economical to produce in other countries. The people of each country can gain by specializing in those things that they can produce at a relatively low cost. For example, countries with warm, moist climates such as Brazil and Colombia find it advantageous to specialize in the production of coffee. People in countries such as Canada and Australia, where land is abundant and population sparse, tend to specialize in land-intensive products, such as wheat, feed grains, and beef. In contrast, in Japan where land is scarce and there is a highly skilled labor force, the Japanese specialize in manufacturing such items as cameras, automobiles, and electronic products for export. As the result of this specialization and trade, aggregate output increases and people in each country are able to achieve a higher standard-of-living than would otherwise be possible.

Second, international trade allows both domestic producers and consumers to gain from reductions in per-unit costs that often accompany large-scale production, marketing, and distribution. This point is particularly important for small countries. With trade, domestic producers can operate on a larger scale and therefore achieve lower per-unit costs than would be possible if they were solely dependent on their domestic market. For example, textile manufacturers in Hong Kong, Taiwan, and South Korea would have much higher per-unit costs if they were unable to sell abroad. The domestic textile market of these countries would be too small to support large, low-cost firms in this industry. With international trade, however, textile firms in these countries are able to produce (and sell) large outputs and compete quite effectively in the world market.

International trade also benefits domestic consumers by permitting them to purchase from large-scale producers abroad. The aircraft industry provides a vivid illustration of this point. Given the huge designing and engineering costs, the domestic market of almost all countries would be substantially less than the quantity required for the efficient production of jet planes. With international trade, however, consumers around the world are able to purchase planes economically from a large-scale producer, such as Boeing or McDonnell-Douglas.

Third, international trade promotes competition in domestic markets and allows consumers to purchase a wide variety of goods at economical prices. Competition from abroad helps keep domestic producers on their toes. It forces them to improve the quality of their products and keep costs low. At the same time, the variety of goods that are available from abroad provides consumers with a much broader array of choices than would be available in the absence of international trade.

The recent experience of the U.S. automobile industry illustrates this point. Faced with stiff competition from Japanese firms, U.S. automobile manufacturers worked hard to improve the quality of their vehicles. As a result, the reliability of the automobiles and light trucks available to American consumers—including those vehicles produced by domestic manufacturers—is almost certainly higher than would have been the case in the absence of competition from abroad.

When countries impose tariffs, quotas, exchange rate controls, bureaucratic regulations on importers or exporters, or other types of trade restraints, they increase transaction costs and reduce the gains from exchange. As Henry George noted (see above quote), trade restraints are like a blockade that a nation imposes on its own people. Just as a blockade imposed by an enemy will harm a nation, so too will a self-imposed blockade in the form of trade restrictions.

Exhibit 4 presents data on the relationship between trade restrictions and economic growth during the 1980s for eighteen less developed countries—eight with low trade restrictions and ten with high trade restrictions. The eight low-restriction countries had relatively low tariff rates (taxes on international trade), and they reduced their tariff rates during the 1980s. For the most part, the low-restriction countries also refrained from the use of exchange rate controls. Thus, the black market premium for currency conversion was either nonexistent or quite small. Reflecting the fact that trade barriers were low, the size of the international trade sector for each of the eight low-restriction countries was large, compared to other countries of similar size. The annual growth rate of per capita income for the low-restriction countries was 5 percent during the 1980-90 period.

Now look at the data for the ten countries that imposed substantial restrictions on international trade. The tariff rates of the high-restriction countries were generally greater than 10 percent, approximately four times the rates imposed by the low-restriction countries. Exchange rate controls resulted in a black market currency conversion premium of 50 percent or more in six (Iran, Brazil, Peru, Bangladesh, Argentina, and Sierra Leone) of the high-restriction countries. Compared to countries of similar size, the international trade sector was small for each of the ten high-restriction countries. On average, the per capita income of the ten high-restriction countries was unchanged during the 1980s. Per capita GDP declined in six of the ten countries. Only two (India and Pakistan) were able to achieve a growth rate equal to that of a low-restriction country. Thus while the low-restriction countries prospered, the high-restriction countries stagnated.

Noneconomists often argue that import restrictions can create jobs. When analyzing this view, once again it is important to keep in mind that it is production that really matters, not jobs. With free trade, domestic consumers are permitted to buy whatever they want wherever they can get the lowest prices. Similarly, domestic producers are able to sell their products wherever they can get the highest prices. The result is that consumers get more for their money and resource owners produce more goods and services that people value. If jobs were the key to high incomes, we could easily create as many as we wanted. All of us could work one day digging holes and the next day filling them up. We would all be employed, but we would also be exceedingly poor because such jobs would not generate goods and services that people value.

Exhibit 4: The Economic Growth of Less Developed Countries with Low and High Trade Restrictions

	Average Tax Rate on International Trade		Black Market Exchange Rate Premium, 1988[a]	Annual Growth of Per Capita GDP 1980-90
	1980	1989		
Low Trade Restrictions				
Singapore	0.5	0.2	0	4.2
Hong Kong	0.0	0.0	0	5.7
Malaysia	7.7	3.2	0	2.6
Ireland	3.0	2.5	2	2.9
Taiwan	3.6	2.2	1	6.5
Thailand	6.9	5.2	1	5.8
South Korea	4.1	3.0	10	8.6
Indonesia	2.9	2.2	16	3.7
Average Growth Rate				**5.0**
High Trade Restrictions				
Iran	8.5	14.6	1030	−1.2
Brazil	10.0	5.5	57	0.5
India	15.5	21.6	14	3.2
Peru	10.6	5.0	240	−2.6
Bangladesh	13.4	12.1	318	2.0
Rwanda	13.3	n.a	30	−2.3
Argentina	9.5	7.0	50	−1.7
Sierra Leone	13.3	11.8	1406	−0.9
Pakistan	15.3	16.1	10	3.2
Ghana	17.3	11.4	36	−0.4
Average Growth Rate				**0.0**

n.a. indicates the data are not available.

[a] A sizeable black market exchange rate premium indicates that the country has imposed exchange rate controls that substantially limit the ability of domestic citizens to convert the national currency to other currencies.

Source: Derived from World Bank, *World Tables, 1991,*and *World Development Report, 1992*; International Money Fund, *Government Finance Yearbook, 1991;* and International Currency Analysis, *The World Currency Yearbook, 1989-90.*

Of course, import restrictions may expand employment in industries shielded by the restraints. This does not mean that they expand total employment, however.

Exports provide the purchasing power for imports. When Americans erect tariffs, quotas, and other barriers limiting the ability of foreigners to sell in the United States, they are simultaneously limiting the ability of foreigners to buy goods produced in the United States. If foreigners are unable to sell as much to Americans, they will have fewer of the dollars required to buy from Americans. Thus, import restrictions will indirectly reduce exports. Output and employment in export industries will decline, offsetting any "jobs saved" in the protected industries. In essence, import restraints direct resources away from areas where domestic firms are low-cost producers and into areas where the domestic firms are high-cost producers. Thus, more of our resources will be employed producing things that we do poorly and fewer will be employed doing those things that we do best. Such policies waste resources and reduce domestic incomes.

Many Americans believe that trade restrictions are necessary to protect U.S. workers from imported goods produced by cheap labor. This view is also false. Countries export goods to us so they can acquire dollars with which to buy from us. The *relative* prices of goods will determine the direction of this trade. High-wage countries will tend to import things that are relatively cheap abroad and export goods that are relatively cheap at home. Therefore, a high-wage country like the United States will tend to import labor-intensive goods, such as wigs, rugs, toys, textiles, and assembled manufactured products. On the other hand, it will tend to export goods like computers, aircraft, scientific instruments, and grains, that are produced with high-skill labor and fertile farm land, resources that are relatively abundant in the United States.

The economy of Hong Kong is probably the freest in the world. Hong Kong has low taxes, no quotas or tariffs, and virtually no restraints on entry into business. Since the mid-1960s the per capita income of Hong Kong has doubled every 12 years. Hong Kong now faces a troublesome issue: Will the unification with China destroy the goose that lays the golden eggs?

When a country can get a product more cheaply from foreigners than it can produce the good domestically, it can gain by importing the product and using domestic resources to produce other things. Perhaps an extreme example will illustrate this point. Suppose a foreign producer such as a Santa Claus who pays workers little or nothing, were willing to supply Americans with free winter coats. Would it make sense to enact a tariff barrier to keep out the free coats? Of course not. Resources that were previously used to produce coats could now be freed to produce other goods. Output and the availability of goods would expand. It makes no more sense to erect trade barriers to keep out cheap foreign goods than to keep out the free coats of a friendly, foreign Santa Claus.

If the "job savers" and proponents of trade restraints think such policies are a good idea, why don't they favor tariffs and quotas limiting trade among the states of the

United States? After all, think of all of the jobs lost when, for example, Michigan "imports" oranges from Florida, apples from Washington, wheat from Kansas, and cotton from Georgia. All of these products could be produced in Michigan. However, the residents of Michigan generally find it cheaper to "import" these commodities rather than produce them locally. Michigan gains by using its resources to produce and "export" automobiles. In turn, the auto sales generate the purchasing power that makes it possible for people from Michigan to "import" goods that would be expensive for them to produce locally.

Most people recognize that free trade among the 50 states is a major source of prosperity for each of the states. They recognize that "imports" from other states do not destroy jobs; they merely release workers for employment in "export" industries, where they will be able to produce more value and therefore generate more income. The underlying source of gains from trade among nations is exactly the same as for trade among people in different states. If free trade among the 50 states promotes prosperity, so too will free trade among nations.

If trade restraints retard economic prosperity, why do so many countries adopt them? The answer is straightforward: the political power of special interests. Trade restrictions benefit producers (and resource suppliers) at the expense of consumers. In general, the former group—investors and workers in a specific industry—are well organized and highly visible, while consumers are generally poorly organized and their gains are more widely dispersed. Predictably, the organized interest group will have more political clout—more votes and more campaign funds. Thus, politicians will often cater to their views. In the case of trade restrictions, sound economics often conflicts with a winning political strategy.

PART III:

Economic Progress and The Role of Government

TEN ELEMENTS OF CLEAR THINKING ABOUT ECONOMIC PROGRESS AND THE ROLE OF GOVERNMENT

1. When Government Protects the Rights of Individuals and Supplies Goods that Cannot Be Provided Through Markets, It Helps Promote Economic Progress.

2. Government is *Not* a Corrective Device.

3. The Cost of Government Is: (a) the Decline in Private Sector Output as the Result of Government's Use of Resources, (b) the Cost of Tax Compliance, and (c) the Unrealized Gains from Exchanges Squeezed Out by Government.

4. Unless Restrained by Constitutional Rules, Special Interest Groups Will Use the Democratic Political Process to Fleece Taxpayers and Consumers.

5. Unless Restrained by Constitutional Rules, Legislators Will Run Budget Deficits that are Often Harmful to the Economy.

6. When Government Becomes Heavily Involved Attempting to Help Some People at the Expense of Others, Resources Will Move Away from Production and Toward Plunder.

7. The Cost of Government Income Transfers Will Be Far Greater Than the Net Gain to the Intended Beneficiaries.

8. Government Central Planning of an Economy Merely Substitutes Politics for Markets; Such an Effort Will Waste Resources and Retard Economic Progress.

9. Competition is Just as Important in Government as in Markets. Competition Among Government Units and Between Government Enterprises and Private Organizations Will Help Assure that Government is a Servant of the People.

10. Constitutional Rules that Bring the Political Process and Sound Economics into Harmony Will Promote Economic Progress.

1. When Government Protects the Rights of Individuals and Supplies Goods that Cannot Be Provided Through Markets, It Helps Promote Economic Progress.

A wise and frugal government, which shall restrain men from injuring one another, which shall leave them otherwise free to regulate their own pursuits of industry and improvements, and shall not take from the mouth of labor the bread it has earned.... This is the sum of good government.

—Thomas Jefferson
(in a letter to Andrew Jackson)

There are two primary ways that a government can promote social cooperation and enhance economic welfare: (a) provide people with protection for their lives, liberties, and properties (as long as they were acquired without force, fraud, or theft) and (b) supply a few select goods that have unusual characteristics that make them difficult to provide through markets. Nobel laureate James Buchanan refers to these functions as the protective and productive functions of government.

The protective function encompasses the government's maintenance of a framework of security and order, including the enforcement of rules against theft, fraud, and the use of violence. Government is assigned a monopoly on the legitimate use of force in order to protect citizens from each other and from outsiders. Thus, the protective state seeks to prevent individuals from harming one another and to maintain an infrastructure of rules within which people can interact with one another harmoniously. The crucial ingredients of this infrastructure include the enforcement of contracts and the avoidance of restrictions, regulations, and differential taxes that would restrain exchange.

It is easy to see the economic importance of this function. When government performs its protective

70

function well, individuals can have confidence that they will not be cheated and that wealth they create will not be taken from them by either selfish intruders or the government via high taxes and the ravages of inflation. Simply put, this protection provides citizens with assurance that if they sow, they will be permitted to reap. When this is true, people will sow and reap abundantly.

On the other hand, when a government performs its protective function poorly, problems arise. If private ownership rights are not clearly defined and enforced, predictably some parties will engage in harmful actions toward others. They will take property that does not belong to them and use resources without paying for them. When people are allowed to impose such costs on non-consenting parties, the "true" cost of producing goods will not be accurately registered by markets. Simultaneously, the resources for which property rights are poorly defined and enforced will tend to be over-utilized. Pollution is a common side-effect. Clearly, the protective function of government is vitally important.

The second primary function of government—the productive function—involves the provision of what economists call *public goods*. Such goods have two distinguishing characteristics: (1) supplying them to one individual simultaneously makes them available to others and (2) it is difficult if not impossible to restrict their consumption to paying customers only. National defense, flood control projects, and mosquito abatement programs provide examples of public goods.

It is extremely difficult for private businesses to produce and market public goods. It is easy to see why. Since the nature of a public good makes it impossible for a private business to establish a one-to-one link between payment and receipt of the good, the customer has little incentive to buy the good. Why would you want to buy it? After all, if others buy, you can consume the good without paying anything for it. Consider the case of a flood-control project. If a firm builds a dam to control flooding, it will be difficult if not impossible to provide the flood control to paying customers while withholding it from nonpaying customers. Recognizing this difficulty, the potential beneficiaries are generally unwilling to help cover the cost of the project. Everybody has an incentive to let "the other guy" pay. When this happens, however, the project may not be undertaken even if it is productive.

In the case of public goods, citizens may be able to gain if they undertake the potentially productive public good projects through government. In essence, activities of this type are what Abraham Lincoln had in mind when he stated his famous dictum that the legitimate function of government is to do those things that people cannot do at all, or cannot do very well, acting in their separate and individual capacities.

How can we tell if a government project is really productive? People have a tendency to believe that support by a majority makes a political action productive or legitimate. Perhaps surprising to some, if a government project is really productive, it will always be possible to allocate the project's cost so that *all* voters will gain. Consider the following benefits received and costs paid by voters from a project—perhaps the construction of a road:

| Voter | Benefits Received | Tax Payment | |
		Plan A	Plan B
Adams	$20	$5	$12.50
Brown	12	5	7.50
Green	4	5	2.50
Jones	2	5	1.25
Smith	2	5	1.25
TOTAL	$40	$25	$25.00

The project costs $25 and generates $40 of benefits for the voters. Since the benefits exceed the costs, the project is productive. If the project's $25 cost is allocated equally among the voters (Plan A), Adams and Brown gain substantially, but Green, Jones, and Smith will lose. The value of the project to the latter three voters is less than their $5 cost. If the fate of the project were decided by majority vote, the project would be defeated by the "no" votes of Green, Jones, and Smith.

In contrast, look what happens if the cost of the project is allocated among voters in proportion to the benefits they received (Plan B). Under this arrangement, Adams would pay half ($12.50) of the $25 cost, since he receives half ($20) of the total benefits ($40). The other voters would all pay in proportion to their benefits received. Under this finance plan, all voters would gain from the proposal. Even though the proposal could not muster a majority when the costs were allocated equally among voters, it would be favored by all five voters if they were taxed in proportion to the benefits that they received (Plan B).

This simple illustration highlights an extremely important point about voting and productive projects. *When voters pay in proportion to the benefits received*, all voters will gain if the government action is productive (and all will lose if it is unproductive).[10] When the benefits and costs of voters are directly related, productive government action will be favored by huge majorities. Correspondingly, support by a supramajority, say 80 or 90 percent of the voters, is strong evidence that the project is productive. Conversely, if a supramajority cannot be achieved, this is strong evidence that the project is counterproductive when the cost-sharing among voters is closely related to the benefits received. Since truly productive projects will tend to be favored by the overwhelming bulk of citizens, many economists believe that taxpayer funds would be spent more productively if a supramajority were required for the approval of each government expenditure program.

2. Government is *Not* a Corrective Device.

People often have a tendency to think of government, particularly a democratically elected government, as a corrective device. They act as if government intervention will solve all types of problems (for example, poverty, inadequate health care, poor education, or the high cost of housing). This view is false. Government is *not* an entity that will always make decisions in the "public interest," however that nebulous term might be defined. Neither is it a corrective device available for use when market organization fails to achieve a desired outcome.

Government is merely a method of social organization— an institutional process through which individuals collectively make choices and carry out activities. There is no assurance that a policy favored by a majority of elected officials will promote economic progress. In fact, there is good reason to expect that, unless the impulses of. the majority are restrained, even popularly elected governments will often adopt policies that undermine economic prosperity.

Many people equate political democracy with a market economy. It is true that most countries that have market economies also have democratic political institutions. However, this is not always the case. For example, even though Hong Kong has a dynamic market economy, it has been under the political control of the British for almost a century. Similarly, while Singapore, South Korea, and Chile have had growing market economies in recent years, the political regimes of these countries have sometimes been oppressive and authoritarian. Conversely, a political democracy does not always guarantee a market economy. Several democratic countries rely extensively on government edicts and tax-expenditure policies rather than markets to allocate goods and resources. Israel and India provide examples.

It is also important to recognize the fundamental differences between political democracy and markets. When a democratic government levies taxes in order to finance government provision of a good, coercion is involved. Dissenting minorities have to pay taxes to finance the good regardless of whether they receive it or value it. The power to tax allows a government to take property (for example, income) from individuals without their permission. There is no such parallel coercive power in the private sector. Private firms can charge a high price, but they cannot force anyone to buy. Indeed, private firms must provide customers with value, or otherwise they will be unable to attract the consumer's dollar. This is not always true with government. When government bureaus or business firms are financed or subsidized by taxes, there is no assurance that people value the output more than its costs.

Unconstrained political democracy is a system of majority rule, while market allocation is a system of proportional representation. When decisions are made through government, if the majority wants more spending on group housing, apartments in the central city, or sex education in public school, the minority must yield and pay the assigned costs. In contrast, the market allows various groups to vote for and receive what they want. For example, when schooling is allocated through the market, some parents choose schools that stress religious values, while others opt for secularism in education. Still others select schools that emphasize basic skills, or cultural diversity, or vocational preparation. With markets, each of these diverse preferences can be satisfied. One need not be a member of the majority; even small minorities are able to "vote" with their consumer dollars and get what they want. As long as any individual or group is willing to pay the cost, the market will respond to their preferences. Each is represented in proportion to the size of their purchases. Conflicts that arise when choices are made in the public sector are avoided.

3. The Cost of Government is: (a) the Decline in Private Sector Output as the Result of Government's Use of Resources, (b) the Cost of Tax Compliance, and (c) the Unrealized Gains from Exchanges Squeezed Out by Government.

Politicians often speak as if taxes are the cost of government. The cost of any product is what we have to give up in order to produce it. Government is no exception. There are three types of costs incurred when governments provide goods and services.

First, there is the loss of private sector output that could have been produced with the resources that are now employed producing the goods supplied by the government. The resources that go into police protection, highways, missiles, education, health care, or any other government "product" have alternative uses. If they were not tied up producing goods supplied through the public sector, they would be available to the private sector. Note that this cost is incurred regardless of whether public-sector goods are financed by current taxes, an increase in government debt, or money creation. It can only be diminished by reducing the size of government purchases.

Second, there is the cost of the resources used to collect taxes and comply with tax legislation: tax returns must be prepared and monitored; tax laws must be enforced. Resources used for these purposes are unavailable for the production of other things in either the private or public sector. In the United States, studies indicates that it takes businesses and individuals approximately 5.5 billion worker-hours (the equivalent of 2,750,000 full-time workers) each year just to complete the taxation paperwork. This compliance cost adds approximately 15 cents to every dollar of tax revenue raised by the government.

Finally, there is the "excess burden" cost due to price distortions resulting from taxes (and borrowing). As a result of taxes, some otherwise mutually advantageous exchanges will become unprofitable, and therefore they will be forsaken. Forgoing these potential gains will impose a cost on the economy. In other cases, taxes may induce individuals to allocate more time to leisure or non-market activities. This, too, will reduce output. Still other taxes will induce people to engage in counter-productive tax avoidance activities, which will impose an additional cost on the economy.

Thus, government purchases cost substantially more than the tax bill or level of expenditures. These costs should be considered when analyzing the merits of government programs.

It is also important to recognize that politicians will attempt to conceal the cost of government. As Senate

"THIS NEW TAX PLAN SOUNDS PRETTY GOOD... WE GET A 9% CUT AND BUSINESS PICKS UP THE BURDEN...."

Republican Leader Robert Dole put it, "Taxing is much like plucking a goose. It is the art of getting the greatest number of feathers with the least amount of hissing."[11] The political attractiveness of budget deficits, money creation, and various indirect taxes stems from the desire of politicians to conceal the costs of government programs.

The deception with regard to business taxes is particularly widespread. Politicians often speak of imposing taxes on "business" as if part of the tax burden could be transferred from individuals to a non-person (business). Purely and simply, business taxes, like all other taxes are paid by individuals. A corporation or business firm may write the check to the government, but it does not pay the taxes. The business firm merely collects the money from someone else—its customers, employees, or stockholders— and transfers it to the government. It may be good political rhetoric to talk about "business" taxes, but the fact is that taxes and all other costs of government are paid for by people.

4. Unless Restrained by Constitutional Rules, Special Interest Groups Will Use the Democratic Political Process to Fleece Taxpayers and Consumers.

When public policy is limited within its proper boundary, government can contribute mightily to economic prosperity. However, this will require more than majority rule and the popular election of legislators.

Unfortunately, democratically elected officials can often gain by supporting policies that favor special interest groups at the expense of the general public. Consider a policy that generates substantial personal gain for the members of a well-organized group (for example, industrial interests, members of a labor union, or farmers) at the expense of the broader interests of taxpayers or consumers. While there are not so many members of the organized interest group, *individually* their personal gain is large. In contrast, while the people who are harmed are many, the cost imposed on each is small and the source of the cost is often difficult to identify.

For issues of this type, it is easy to see why politicians often support special interest groups. Since the personal stake of the interest group members is substantial, they have a strong incentive to form alliances and let candidates and legislators know how strongly they feel about the issue. Many interest group members will condition both their vote and financial support almost exclusively on the basis of where a politician stands on issues of special importance to them. On the other hand, since a special interest issue exerts only a small personal impact on other voters, the bulk of voters will often be uninformed and generally care little about such an issue.

If you are a vote-seeking politician what would you do? Clearly, little gain would be derived from supporting the interest of the largely uninformed and disinterested majority, but vocal supporters, campaign workers, and most importantly, campaign contributions can be derived from the support of the policies favored by the special interests. In the age of media politics, there is strong pressure for politicians to support special interests, tap them for campaign funds, and use the contributions to project a positive candidate image on television. Politicians unwilling to play this game—those unwilling to use the government treasury to provide well-organized interest groups with favors in exchange for political support—are seriously disadvantaged. Given the current rules, politicians are led as if by an invisible hand to reflect the views of special interest groups, even though this often leads to wasteful policies.

The bottom line is clear: representative government based solely on majority rule does not handle special interest issues well. The tendency of the unrestrained political process to favor well-organized groups helps explain the presence of many programs that reduce the size of the economic pie. For example, consider the case of the roughly 33,000 rice farmers in the United States. In essence, the government guarantees rice growers an above market price for rice by paying them to grow less, so the artificially high price can be maintained. The program reduces output, pushes up the price of rice, and results in higher taxes. Nonetheless, Congress continues to support the program. The rice farmers gain more than $800 million in gross income, approximately $25,000 per rice farm. More than 60 percent of these subsidies go to rice farmers receiving payments of $50,000 or more.

Given the sizable impact on their personal wealth, it is perfectly sensible for rice farmers to use their votes, contributions and political influence to help politicians who support their interests. In contrast, it makes no sense for the average voter to investigate this issue or give it any significant weight when deciding for whom to vote. In fact, most Americans are unaware that they pay approximately $4 more per year to help rice growers, most of which goes to wealthy farmers. As a result, politicians can generally gain by continuing to support the rice farmers even though the subsidy program wastes resources and reduces the wealth of the nation.

The fleecing of taxpayers and consumers in order to provide benefits to identifiable and politically active voting blocs has become the primary business of modern politics. Taxpayers and consumers spend approximately $20 billion annually to support grain, cotton, tobacco, peanut, wool, and dairy programs, all of which have the same structure as the rice program. The political power of special interests also explains the presence of tariffs and quotas on steel, shoes, brooms, textiles, and several other products. Regulations mandating that Alaskan oil be transported by the high-cost American maritime industry reflect the industry's political clout, not its economic efficiency. Federally-funded irrigation projects, subsidized agricultural grazing rights, subsidized business loans, subsidies to airports—the list goes on and on. Each of these policies is rooted in the special interest effect rather than sound economic doctrine. While each such program individually imposes only a small drag on our economy, in the aggregate they bust the federal budget, waste resources, and lower the standard of living of Americans.

The framers of the U.S. Constitution were aware of this defect of democratic politics (they called the interest groups "factions"). The Constitution sought to limit pressure from the factions in Article I, Section 8, which specifies that Congress is to levy only *uniform* taxes for programs that promote the *common* defense and *general* welfare. This clause was designed to preclude the use of general tax revenue to provide benefits to sub-groups of the population. However, through the years court decisions and legislative acts have gutted and distorted its meaning. Thus, as it is currently interpreted, the Constitution is no longer able to constrain the political power of well-organized special interest groups.

5. Unless Restrained by Constitutional Rules, Legislators Will Run Budget Deficits that are Often Harmful to the Economy.

When the spending of a government exceeds its revenues, a *budget deficit* results. In 1992, the federal budget deficit of the United States was $295 billion. Governments generally issue interest-earning bonds to finance their budget deficits. By year end 1992, the U.S. Treasury had approximately $4.1 trillion of bonds outstanding. These outstanding obligations are often referred to as the *national debt*. When the government runs a budget deficit, it increases the size of the national debt.

Deficit spending has become a way of life for modern governments. During the 1970s and 1980s, the central governments of every major industrial country consistently ran budget deficits. In turn, the deficits pushed up the national debt. As Exhibit 5 shows, the net national debt of the United States has been increasing as a percent of Gross Domestic Product (GDP) since 1973.

The source of the deficits is hardly a mystery. Legislators like to spend money on programs to please their constituents. On the other hand, they do not like to tax, since taxes impose a visible cost on voters. Debt is an alternative to *current* taxes—it pushes the *visible* cost of government into the future.

What impact does debt-financing have on the economy? Do deficits harm future generations? Some argue that debt-financing permits us to have a party today and send the bill to our grandchildren. Clearly, this view overstates the case. The ability of debt to shift the cost of government into the future is limited. In the United States, most of the government debt is owed to Americans. Americans will

Exhibit 5: Net National Debt as a Percent of GDP for the United States—1950 to 1991

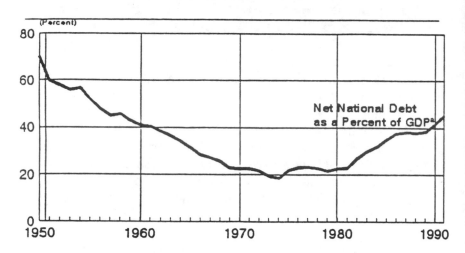

The net national debt omits that portion of the national debt that is held by federal government agencies and the Federal Reserve Bank.

Source: *Economic Report of the President* (various issues).

have to pay higher taxes to meet the interest payments on the national debt. At the same time, however, most of the interest income will be received by Americans. Thus, in the case of domestically held debt, our children and grandchildren will both pay the taxes to service the debt and receive the interest payments.

When current resources are used to produce government services, these resources will not be available to produce other things. This will be true regardless of whether the government finances these services with debt or taxes. For example, when the government builds a highway, it draws resources with alternative uses away from the private sector. *Current* output of goods for private consumption and investment will decline as a result of the government's use of resources . This cost is incurred in the present; debt financing cannot push it into the future.

Does this mean that there is little reason to be concerned about an adverse impact of deficits on future generations? Not necessarily. Debt-financing influences future generations primarily through its potential impact on savings and capital formation. If the current generation leaves lots of factories, machines, houses, knowledge, and other productive assets to its children, then the productive potential of the next generation will be high. Alternatively, if fewer productive assets (and more government bonds) are passed along to the next generation, then their productive capability will decline accordingly. Thus, the true measure of how government debt influences future generations involves knowledge of its impact on capital formation.

Most economists believe that government borrowing to finance a deficit pushes interest rates upward. These higher interest rates will, in turn, crowd out private investment. If the government used the borrowed funds for investment, additional government investment would help to offset the decline in private investment. But this is generally not the case. Most government spending in industrial countries goes for income transfers, business subsidies, and other things that provide immediate benefits to organized groups. Thus, the budget deficit almost certainly reduces the capital stock (tools, machines, and factories) available to future generations. As a result, the productivity and wages of future workers will be lower than would be true in the absence of the deficits.

If the deficits are not controlled, could they cause an economic collapse? When considering this view, it is important to recognize that borrowing is a standard method of doing business. Many large and profitable corporations continually have debt outstanding. As long as the net income of a business firm is large relative to its interest liability, the outstanding debt poses little problem. So it is with the federal government. As long as people have confidence that it can raise the tax revenue necessary

Exhibit 6: Net Interest Cost as a Percent of Federal Revenue for United States—1950 to 1991

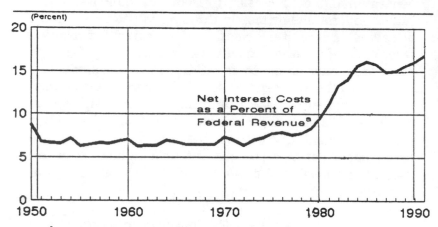

* The net interest costs include only the interest paid to private investors. The interest on debt held by federal government agencies and Federal Reserve Banks is omitted.

Source: *Economic Report of the President* (various issues).

to meet its debt obligations, the federal government will have no trouble financing and refinancing its outstanding debt.

Thus, the key to credit-worthiness is expected future income relative to interest liability. This is true for individuals, private businesses, and governments. What is happening to the credit-worthiness of the U.S. federal government? In the late 1940s, approximately 10 percent of U.S. federal revenues went to pay the interest on the national debt. As Exhibit 6 illustrates, net interest costs were approximately 7 percent of federal revenues throughout the 1951–1974 period. Since that time, interest costs as a share of federal revenues have risen, soaring to 14 percent in 1983 and 17 percent in 1991.

This is a trend that cannot continue, at least not without serious consequences. If the interest costs continue to rise relative to federal revenues, people will become increasingly fearful that the government might resort to "printing-press" money in an effort to escape its loan obligations. If this should happen, the fear of rapid money growth and inflation would push interest rates up and make it even more difficult for the government to meet its debt obligations. If sufficiently intense, the fear of inflation alone could seriously disrupt the long-term capital market not only for the federal government, but for other borrowers as well. And if the government did resort to "printing press" money in order to pay off its debt, hyperinflation and a breakdown in the exchange system would result. The economy would be severely crippled.

Excessive debt has led to financial crises elsewhere. The economies of several countries, including Bolivia, Argentina, Chile, Brazil, and Israel have been ravaged in recent years by excessive debt, money creation, and runaway inflation. If the interest liability of the federal government continued to grow more rapidly than revenues, clearly the United States would not be immune to such an occurrence.

What needs to be done? The "deficit problem" is a political structure problem. Deficit spending is a natural outgrowth of unrestrained democratic politics. Borrowing allows politicians to supply voters with *immediate* benefits without having to impose a parallel visible cost in the form of higher taxes or user charges. If unconstrained by constitutional rules or strong convictions, predictably politicians will use deficits to partially conceal the cost of their programs from voters.

The unconstrained political process plays into the hands of well-organized interest groups and encourages "pork-barrel" spending. Each representative has a strong incentive to fight hard for expenditures beneficial to his or her constituents and little incentive to oppose spending by others. A legislator who is a spending "watch dog" will incur the wrath of colleagues favoring special programs for their districts. More importantly, the benefits (for example, tax reductions and lower interest rates) of spending cuts and deficit reductions will be spread thinly among the voters in all districts. Thus, the legislator's constituents will reap only a small part of these benefits.

It is as if 535 families go out to dinner knowing that after the meal each will receive a bill for 1/535th of the cost. No family feels compelled to order less, because their restraint will exert little impact on the total bill. Why not order shrimp for an appetizer, entrees of steak and lobster, and a large piece of cheesecake for dessert? After all, the extra spending will add only a few pennies to each family's share of the total bill. However, when everybody follows this course of action, many items are purchased that are valued less than their cost.[12]

So it is with congressional decisionmaking. Representatives have a strong incentive to push for programs helpful to their own districts, particularly when each recognizes that other legislators are doing so. Similarly, they have a strong incentive to conceal the cost of government programs from voters. Given this incentive structure, large budget deficits are the expected occurrence.

Would a tax increase reduce the budget deficit? For example, would a $50 billion tax increase reduce the deficit of the United States? The answer is almost certainly "No!" A 1991 study prepared for the Joint Economic Committee of Congress found that since 1947, every new dollar of tax revenue generated spending increases of $1.59! Thus additional revenue led to even greater spending increases. In 1982 President Reagan agreed to a highly publicized tax increase if Congress would cut spending. Taxes were increased, but the spending cuts failed to materialize. Former President Bush fell into the same trap with his infamous 1990 budget agreement. Once again, taxes were raised, spending increased more than was projected, and the budget deficit expanded. Given the current political structure, there is little reason to believe that higher taxes will reduce the deficit. Congress will spend every dollar it can get its hands on, plus a few hundred billion more!

If we are really going to do something about the deficit, we will have to modify the political structure. The rules need to be changed, so it will be more difficult for politicians to spend more than they are willing to tax. There are several ways this might be done. The Constitution might be amended to require the federal government to balance its budget, even as most state governments are required to balance their budgets. A constitutional amendment requiring two thirds or three-fourths approval of both houses for spending proposals and increases in the federal government's borrowing power might be sought. This year's spending might be limited to last year's level of revenues. Proposed rule changes of this type would make it more difficult for legislators to spend, unless they were willing to tax or charge for the government services. Such rule changes would stiffen up the government's budget constraint, reduce the power of special interests, and discourage "pork-barrel" politics. They would also force legislators to consider more carefully the costs of government programs. An improvement in the cost-effectiveness of government would surely result.

6. When Government Becomes Heavily Involved Attempting to Help Some People at the Expense of Others, Resources Will Move Away from Production and Toward Plunder. Economic Progress Will Be Retarded.

The tool of politics (which frequently becomes its objective) is to extract resources from the general taxpayer with minimum offense and to distribute the proceeds among innumerable claimants in such a way to maximize the support at the polls. Politics, so far as mobilizing support is concerned, represents the art of calculated cheating—or more precisely, how to cheat without being really caught.[13]

—James R. Schlesinger
Secretary of Defense, 1973-75

There are two ways individuals can acquire wealth: production and plunder. People can get ahead by producing things (or services) and exchanging them for income. This method of acquiring income both helps the trading partners and enhances the wealth of society. But sometimes the rules also allow people to get ahead by "plundering" what others have produced. This method not only fails to generate additional income—the gain of one is a loss to another—but it also consumes resources and thereby reduces the wealth of the society.

Governments promote economic prosperity when they encourage productive activity and discourage plunder. This objective can best be achieved by a government that acts as a neutral force, protecting property rights and enforcing contracts. When the effective law of the land makes it difficult to take the property of others, few resources will flow into plunder.

In the modern world, government itself is often used as an agent for plunder. The quantity of resources directed toward lobbying, political campaigns, and the various forms of "favor-seeking" from the government will be directly proportional to the ease with which the political process can be used for personal (or interest group) gain at the expense of others. When a government fails to allocate the cost of public sector projects to the primary beneficiaries (through user fees, for example) or when it becomes heavily involved in income transfer activities, people will spend more time organizing and lobbying politicians and less time producing goods and services.[14] Resources that would otherwise be used to create wealth and generate income are wasted fighting over slices of a shrinking economic pie.

In this era of the unconstrained state, income transfers from taxpayers to well-organized groups and voting blocs have become the business of modern politics in the wealthy industrial countries of North America and Western Europe. The competitive advantage goes to the politician who can figure out how to get revenues in the least offensive way and then use the funds to favor groups willing to supply the most votes in exchange for the transfers. Counterproductive, favor-seeking activities are a natural outgrowth of unrestrained democracy. Unless democratic governments are constrained constitutionally, politicians will enact programs that waste resources and impair the general standard of living.

7. The Cost of Government Income Transfers Will Be Far Greater Than the Net Gain to the Intended Beneficiaries.

When the War on Poverty was declared in the mid-1960s, it was widely believed that poverty could be eliminated if only Americans were willing to transfer a little more income to the less fortunate members of society. They were, and income transfer programs expanded substantially. *As a proportion of personal income*, transfers directed toward the poor (for example, Aid to Families with Dependent Children, food stamps, and Medicaid) doubled during the 1965–1975 period. Since 1975, the percent of income allocated to transfers has been maintained at the higher level.

The results, however, were quite different from what most people expected. After declining for two decades following the Second World War, the poverty rate of the non-elderly began to rise in the late 1960s, shortly after the transfers were expanded. Twenty-five years after the War on Poverty was initiated, the poverty rate of the non-elderly was slightly *higher* in 1990 than it was in 1965. The poverty rate rose, even though income, adjusted for both inflation and population growth, grew by more than 50 percent between 1965 and 1990.

Why weren't the income transfers more effective? Economic analysis indicates that their ineffectiveness reflects a more general proposition: it is difficult to transfer income to a group of recipients in a manner that will improve their long term well-being. Once again, this proposition reflects the unintended secondary effects of the transfers.[15] Three major factors undermine the effectiveness of income transfers.

First, an increase in the size of the transfer sector will retard economic growth. Income is not like "manna from heaven." Neither is national income an economic pie that is baked by the government so slices of various sizes can be served up hot to people throughout the country. On the contrary, income is something that people produce and earn. It is earned by individuals who provide others with goods and services for which they are willing to pay.

Tax and transfer policies adversely influence both the taxpayer's and the transfer recipient's incentive to earn. As taxes to finance the transfers increase, taxpayers have less incentive to produce and earn and more incentive to invest in wasteful tax shelters. Similarly, since transfer benefits tend to decline as the income of a recipient increases, the recipient will also have less incentive to earn since net income will increase by only a fraction—and in many cases only a small fraction—of the additional earnings. Thus, neither taxpayers nor transfer recipients will produce and earn as much as they would in the absence of the transfer program. In addition, the reallocation of income by politics will encourage people to spend more time politicking and less time producing. All of these factors will retard economic growth, which will tend to reduce the welfare of the intended beneficiaries as well as that of other citizens.

Second, competition for transfers will erode most of the long-term gain of the intended beneficiaries. In a world of scarce resources, governments must establish a criterion for the receipt of income transfers and other political favors. If it did not do so, the transfers would bust the budget. Generally, the government will require a transfer recipient to own something, do something, or be something. However, once a criterion is established, people will modify their behavior to qualify for the "free" money or other government favors. As they do so, their net gain from the transfers declines.

The following thought experiment illustrates this important point. Suppose the U.S. government decided to give away a $50 bill between 9 a.m. and 5 p.m. to all persons willing to wait in line at the teller windows of the U.S. Treasury. Long lines would emerge. How long? How much time would people be willing to take from their leisure and their productive activities? A person whose time was worth $5 per hour would be willing to spend up to 10 hours waiting in line for the $50. Others whose time was worth less, say $3 or $4 per hour, would find that what they had to do in order to get the transfer consumed much of its value.

This simple example illustrates why the intended beneficiaries of transfer programs are not helped much. When beneficiaries have to do something (for example, wait in line, fill out forms, lobby government officials, take an exam, endure delays, or contribute to selected political campaigns) in order to qualify for a transfer, a great deal of their potential gain will be lost as they seek to meet the qualifying criteria. Similarly, when beneficiaries have to own something (for example, land with an acreage allotment to grow wheat, or a license to operate a taxicab or sell a product to foreigners) in order to get a subsidy, people will bid up the price of the asset needed to qualify for the subsidy until the higher asset price captures the value of the subsidy. In each case, the potential beneficiaries will compete to meet the criteria until they largely dissipate the *net* value of the transfer. As a result, the recipient's *net gain* will generally be substantially less than the amount of the transfer payment. This explains why transfer programs have generally failed to upgrade the well being of their intended beneficiaries.

Of course, unanticipated changes in transfer programs can generate temporary gains or losses for various groups. Once a program is institutionalized, however, competition will eliminate abnormally large returns from any activity that increases one's likelihood of qualifying for a government favor.

There is a third reason for the ineffectiveness of transfers: programs that protect potential recipients against adversity arising from their imprudent decisions encourage choices that increase the likelihood of the adversity. The transfers do two things to potential beneficiaries: (a) they make the consequences of the adversity less severe and (b) they reduce the incentive of potential recipients to take steps to avoid the adversity. The problem arises because these two things exert conflicting influences. For example, government subsidies of insurance premiums in hurricane areas will make it less costly for people to protect themselves against economic losses resulting from a hurricane. Since the protection is cheaper, however, people are encouraged to build in hurricane-prone areas. As a result, the damage from hurricanes is greater than would otherwise be the case. Unemployment compensation provides another example. The benefits make it less costly for unemployed workers to refuse existing offers and keep looking for a better job. Therefore, workers engage in longer periods of job search and, as a result, the unemployment rate is higher than would otherwise be the case.

If you subsidize something, you will get more of it. Anti-poverty transfers are no exception to this general rule. Transfers directed toward the poor encourage high-risk lifestyles (for example, the use of drugs, dropping out of school or the workforce, births by single mothers, marital dissolution, and abandonment of children by fathers). All of these choices tend to increase the number of people who are poor. These secondary effects may not be very important in the short term. Over the longer term, however, the unintended negative consequences will be more severe. In addition, the government anti-poverty transfers crowd out private charitable efforts by families, individuals, churches, and civic organizations. When taxes are levied to do more about a problem, private individuals and groups will predictably adjust and do less to alleviate the problem.

From an economic viewpoint, the failure of transfer programs ranging from farm price supports to anti-poverty programs is not surprising. When the secondary effects are considered, economic analysis indicates that it is extremely difficult to help the intended beneficiaries over the long term.

8. Government Central Planning of an Economy Merely Substitutes Politics for Markets; Such an Effort Will Waste Resources and Retard Economic Progress.

The man of system...is apt to be very wise in his own conceit...[H]e seems to imagine that he can arrange the different members of a great society with as much ease as the hand arranges the different pieces upon a chess-board; he does not consider that the pieces upon the chess-board have not another principle of motion besides that which the hand impresses upon them; but that, in the great chess-board of human society, every single piece has a principle of motion of its own, although different from that which the legislature might choose to impress upon it. If those two principles coincide and act in the same direction, the game of human society will go on easily and harmoniously, and is very likely to be happy and successful. If they are opposite or different, the game will go on miserably, and the society must be at all times in the highest degree of disorder.[16]

—Adam Smith (1759)

As previously discussed, governments can often coordinate the production of public goods—a small class of goods for which it is difficult to restrict consumption to paying customers only—better than markets. Government provision of public goods can promote economic progress.

However, many people also believe that government can pick industries, provide subsidies, and direct investments in a way that will accelerate the growth of the economy. According to this view, government "industrial planning" and "investment in future economic growth" can improve on market outcomes. It is easy to see how this view has a certain appeal. Surely, it makes sense to plan. Aren't elected officials and government experts more likely to represent the "general welfare" of the people than business entrepreneurs? Won't government officials be "less greedy" than private businesses? People who do not understand the invisible hand principle often find the argument for central planning persuasive. Economics, however, indicates that it is wrong. There are four major reasons why central planning will almost surely do more damage than good.

First, central planning merely substitutes politics for market verdicts. Remember, government is not a corrective device. Real world central planners (and the legislators who direct them) are not a group of omniscient selfless saints. Predictably, the subsidies and investment funds doled out by planners will be influenced by political considerations.

Think how this process works even when decisions are made democratically. Expenditures will have to be approved by the legislature. Various business and unionized labor interests will lobby for investment funds and subsidies that provide them with benefits. Legislators will be particularly sensitive to those in a position to provide campaign contributions and deliver key voting blocs. Compared to newer "growth" firms, older established businesses will have a stronger record of political contributions, better knowledge of lobbying techniques, and a closer relationship with powerful political figures. As former Senator William Proxmire has said, "The money will go where the political power is." Predictably, elevating the political process will favor older firms, even if they are economically weak, over newer growth-oriented firms. In addition, committee chairmen will often block various programs unless other legislators agree to support "pork-barrel" projects beneficial to their constituents and favored interest groups. Only a hopeless dreamer would believe that this politicized process would result in less waste, more wealth creation, and a better allocation of investment funds than markets.

Second, there is every reason to believe that investors risking their own money will make better investment choices than central planners playing with the money of taxpayers. Remember, if an investor is going to profit, he or she must discover and invest in a project that increases the value of resources. If the investor makes a mistake—if the investment project turns out to be a loser—he or she will bear the consequences directly. In contrast, the link between the selection of productive projects and the personal wealth of the central planners will be weak. Even if a project is productive, the planner's personal gain is likely to be quite modest. Similarly, if the project is wasteful—if it reduces the value of resources—this failure will exert little negative impact on the planners. In fact, they may even be able to reap personal gain from wasteful projects that channel subsidies and other benefits toward politically powerful groups. Given this incentive structure, there is simply no reason to believe that central planners will be more likely than private investors to discover and act on projects that increase wealth.

Third, the central planners will be fed inaccurate information. Knowing that the planners are a source of investment funds and subsidies, managers of both private and public enterprises will supply planners with biased and inaccurate information designed to attract government favors. Predictably, they will try to convince the planners that their enterprise or industry is producing (or could produce) a product or service that is enormously valuable to the general public. If their enterprise were just given more funding, they would do wonderful things for the general well-being of society. On the other hand, if the government favors are not forthcoming, jobs will be lost and local economies will collapse. While the planners may know that these claims are exaggerated, they will often lack the information necessary to evaluate them carefully. This will be particularly true if the supplier is a monopolist.

Fourth, there is no way that central planners can acquire enough information to create a national plan that makes sense. We live in a world of dynamic change. Technological advances, new products, political unrest, changing demand, and shifting weather conditions are constantly altering the relative scarcity of both goods and resources. No central authority will be able to keep up with these changes and provide local enterprise managers with sensible instructions.

Markets register and tabulate widely fragmented information. Prices reflect this widely dispersed information and use it to send signals to business firms and resource suppliers. In turn, these price signals provide businesses and resource owners with the information required to coordinate their actions and bring them into harmony with the new conditions. There is simply no way that even a significant fraction of the relevant but widely dispersed information could be communicated accurately to any individual or central planning agency.

The incredible diversity of the wants and desires of people is well beyond the comprehension of any central planning agency. So, too, is the knowledge of unique local circumstances, elements of timing, and the importance of location. Thus, the planners will be operating with only a small fraction of the relevant information and much of that will be inaccurate by the time it is communicated to them. The view that a single individual or committee could acquire and maintain sufficient information to make sound decisions in our rapidly changing modern world is a delusion. The complex coordination that is the central element of modern economics is simply too complicated to be handled by any central planning authority.

The proponents of planning often point to Japan's Ministry of International Trade and Industry (MITI) as an example of how industrial planning should work. MITI successes have been greatly exaggerated and its failures totally ignored. MITI tried to keep both Mazda and Honda out of the automobile business because it did not think they would be able to compete successfully. It tried to stop Sony from producing transistor radios. MITI has protected high-cost Japanese firms in shipbuilding and mining. Its import restrictions on meat, citrus, and other agricultural products force Japanese consumers to spend far more on food than consumers in other industrial countries. The business success of the Japanese has been in spite of, not because of, MITI's industrial planning.

Similarly, the record of government planning in the United States is fraught with internal inconsistencies. The federal government both subsidizes tobacco growers *and* propagandizes against smoking. It pays some farmers *not* to produce grain products and, at the same time, subsidizes others with irrigation projects so they can grow more of the very same grain products. Government programs for dairy farmers keep the price of milk high, while its subsidies to the school lunch program make the expensive milk more affordable. Government regulations mandating stronger bumpers make automobiles safer, while the government's Corporate Average Fuel Economy (CAFE) standards make them lighter and more dangerous. Both increase the cost of automobiles.

Those who think that central planning will promote economic progress are naive. When business enterprises get more funds from governments and less from consumers, they will spend more time trying to satisfy politicians and less time satisfying customers. Predictably, this reallocation of resources will lead to economic regression rather than prosperity.

9. **Competition is Just as Important in Government as in Markets. Competition Among Government Units and Between Government Enterprises and Private Organizations Will Help Assure that Government is a Servant of the People.**

Competition is a disciplinary force. In the marketplace, businesses must compete for the loyalty of customers. When firms serve their customers poorly, they generally lose business to rivals offering a better deal. Competition provides consumers with protection against high prices, shoddy merchandise, poor service, and/or rude behavior. Almost everyone recognizes this point with regard to the private sector. Unfortunately, the importance of competition in the public sector is not so widely recognized.

The incentive structure confronted by government agencies and enterprises is not very conducive to efficient operation. Unlike private owners, the directors and managers of public sector enterprises are seldom in a position to gain much from lower cost and improved performance. In fact, the opposite is often true. If an agency fails to spend this year's allocation, its case for a larger budget next year is weakened. Thus, agencies typically go on a spending spree at the end of the budget period if they discover that they have failed to spend all of this year's appropriation.

In the private sector, profit rate provides an easily identifiable index of performance. Since there is not a comparable indicator of performance in the public sector, managers of government firms can often gloss over economic inefficiency. In the private sector, bankruptcy eventually weeds out inefficiency. In the public sector, there is no parallel mechanism for the termination of unsuccessful programs. In fact, poor performance and failure to achieve objectives is often used as an argument for *increased* funding in the public sector. For example, if the achievement scores of students are declining, public school administrators will use this failure to argue for increased funding. Similarly, the police department will use a rising crime rate to argue for additional law enforcement funding.

Given the incentive structure within the public sector, it is vitally important that government enterprises face competitors. Prosperity will be enhanced if private firms are permitted to compete on a level playing field with government agencies and enterprises. For example, if governments operate vehicle maintenance departments, printing shops, food services, garbage collection services, street maintenance departments, schools, and similar agencies; private firms could be given an equal opportunity to compete with public enterprises. The competition would improve performance, reduce costs, and stimulate innovative behavior in both sectors. As a result, consumer/ taxpayers would get more for their money.

Competition among decentralized government units will also help promote economic progress. A government cannot be oppressive when it is relatively easy to choose the "exit option"—to move to another location that provides a level of government services and taxes more to your liking. Of course, it is not as easy to walk away from your government as it from your grocer! In a decentralized setting, however, citizens can vote with their feet. If the functions of the central government are strictly limited to the protection of individual rights, prohibition against restraints of trade, and the provision of national defense, then state and local governments can vary widely in the degree to which they tax themselves for the provision of government services. Just as people differ with regard to the amount they want to spend on housing or automobiles, so too will they have different views concerning expenditures on public services. Some will prefer a high level of government services and be willing to pay higher taxes for them. Others will prefer lower taxes and fewer governmental services. Some will want to fund government services with taxes, while others will prefer greater reliance on user charges. A decentralized system can accommodate and satisfy all of these divergent views.

Competition among local governments will also help promote governmental efficiency. When citizens can easily vote with their feet, the incentive of government to provide them with services economically is enhanced. If a government levies high taxes without providing a parallel quality of services, both individuals and businesses will be repelled. Similarly, when people are taxed for things that provide them with little or no value, many will choose the "exit option" and will move to areas where the government provides them "more for their money". Thus, like business firms in the marketplace, local governments that fail to serve their citizens will lose "customers" (population) and revenues.

Competition among decentralized governments serves the interests of the citizen/taxpayer. If it is going to work, however, the policies of the federal government must not stifle it. When a central government subsidizes, mandates, and regulates the bundle of government services provided by local governments, it undermines the competitive process among them. The best thing the central government can do is perform its limited functions well and remain neutral with regard to the operation and level of services of state, regional, and local governments.

Like private enterprises, governments prefer protection from rivals. There will be a tendency for governments to seek a monopoly position. Therefore, competition among governments will not evolve automatically. It will have to be incorporated into the political structure. This is precisely what the American founders were attempting to do when they designed the U.S. Constitution and federal system of the United States.

10. Constitutional Rules that Bring the Political Process and Sound Economics into Harmony Will Promote Economic Progress.

The predominant teachings of this age are that there are no limits to man's capacity to govern others and that, therefore, no limitations ought to be imposed upon government. The older faith, born of long ages of suffering under man's dominion over man, was that the exercise of unlimited power by men with limited minds and self-regarding prejudices is soon oppressive, reactionary, and corrupt. The older faith taught that the very condition of progress was the limitation of power to the capacity and the virtue of rulers. Men may have to pass through a terrible ordeal before they find again the central truths they have forgotten. But they will find them again as they have so often found them again in other ages of reaction, if only the ideas that have misled them are challenged and resisted.[17]

—Walter Lippmann

The intellectual folly of our age is the view that democratic elections alone will establish an environment conducive to economic progress. Both history and political theory indicate that this view is false. If government is going to be a positive force for economic prosperity, the rules of the political game must be designed to bring the self-interest of voters, politicians, and bureaucrats into harmony with economic progress. This will require that the scope of government be limited and that government remain neutral among the various sub-groups of citizens.

When government is unconstrained—when everything is up for grabs within the political process—divisive and predatory activities will abound. Individuals will spend more time organizing and fighting over slices of the economic pie and less time producing "pie." As a result, output will be smaller than would otherwise be the case. Animosity, distrust, and even hatred among factions will grow, while production stagnates. Life in a highly politicized economy is not very pleasant.

The framers of the U.S. Constitution recognized this point and therefore incorporated restraints on the economic role of government. They enumerated the permissible fiscal powers of the central government (Article I, Section 8) and allocated all other powers to the states and the people (Tenth Amendment). They also prohibited states from adopting legislation "impairing the obligation of contracts" (Article I, Section 10). Furthermore, the Fifth Amendment specifies that private property shall not be "taken for public use without just compensation." Clearly, the U.S. Constitution sought to limit the ability of government, particularly the federal government, to politicize the economy and exploit the rights of citizens.

With the passage of time, however, the economic restraints eroded. As a result, the federal government is now involved in almost everything. The secondary effects of this politicized structure are now obvious—high taxes, excessive regulations, special interest spending, and huge budget deficits that threaten our financial structure. The challenge before us is to design constitutional rules and procedures that will help bring the political process back into harmony with economic progress.

A Positive Program for Prosperity

How can this be accomplished? What provisions would a constitution designed to promote economic prosperity and stability contain? Several proposals flow directly from our analysis. Within the American context, we believe the following seven provisions would provide the core for an Economic Bill of Rights that would promote economic progress:

a. *No government shall use its regulatory powers to take private property, either partially or in its entirety, for public use without paying the owner the full market value of the property taken.*

In recent years, state and local governments in particular have used regulations to take private property without compensation. The courts have generally allowed them to do so as long as a legislative body deemed that the action was in the public interest or that the taking did not deny the owner all uses of his or her property. This is an open door to abuse that must be closed.

b. *The right of people to buy and sell legally tradeable goods and services at mutually acceptable terms shall not be infringed by Congress or any of the States.*[18]

Freedom of exchange is a cornerstone of economic progress. Price controls, professional and occupational entry restraints,[19] laws prohibiting trade among people of different racial, ethnic, or religious groups, and other government regulations that restrain trade should be prohibited.

c. *Congress shall not levy taxes or impose quotas on either imports or exports.*

The U.S. Constitution already prohibits the imposition of these trade restraints on exports. This prohibition should also be extended to imports.

d. *A three-fourths approval of both Houses of Congress shall be required for all expenditure programs of the federal government. At least two-thirds approval of the legislative branches of state government shall be required for the approval of expenditures by state governments.*

Remember, if a project is really productive, there will always be a method of finance that will result in everyone gaining (see pages 72-73). Thus, the supramajority provisions need not eliminate projects that truly increase wealth. They will, however, make it more difficult for special interests to use government as a tool for plunder. They will also help keep the spending activities of governments at the local level where competition among governments provides a stronger incentive for governments to serve the interests of all citizens.

e. *A three-fourths approval of both Houses of Congress shall be required before the federal government is permitted to borrow any funds to finance a deficit in its annual budget.*

This will reduce the inclination of Congress to spend beyond its means.

f. *A three-fourths approval of both Houses of Congress shall be required for the federal government to mandate any expenditures by either state governments or private business firms.*

If this provision is not included, Congress will use mandated expenditures to escape the prior spending and borrowing limitations.

g. *The function of the Federal Reserve System is to maintain the value of the currency and establish a stable price level. If the price level either increases or decreases by more than 5 percent annually during two consecutive years, all Governors of the Federal Reserve System shall be required to submit their resignations.*

This provision would make it clear what the Fed is supposed to do. If the Fed establishes monetary stability, it is doing its part to promote economic stability and progress.

Economic analysis indicates that these provisions would help promote economic progress and limit the inclination of politicians to serve special-interest groups. They would be a positive step toward the restoration of government based on mutual agreement rather than the power to plunder.

Before constitutional rules consistent with economic progress can be reestablished, however, the intellectual fabric underlying the case for limited government must be mended. We must cast aside the myth that popular elections are the distinctive feature of the American political process. We must recognize that it is one thing to determine our political leaders by majority vote and quite another to determine what government will do by majority rule. It is limited government, not majority rule, that is the key to economic progress. The sooner we learn this important point, the more prosperous we will be.

Concluding Thoughts

During a visit to the former Soviet Union in 1992, a Russian told one of the authors, "We know what doesn't work; now we are trying to figure out what will work." The Russians are not alone. Much of the world is searching for economic prescriptions that work.

As we have indicated throughout this book, both basic economics and the American experience provide insight into this issue. Basic economics indicates that private ownership, freedom of exchange, competitive markets, and monetary stability are the cornerstones of economic prosperity. When these cornerstones are present, individuals will be able "to reap what they sow," productive energy will be released, and wealth will be created. This is the recipe that generated America's material progress. To the degree that America departs from it, America will cease to experience growth and prosperity.

Moreover, it is a recipe that will work around the world. Countries that adopt sound policies will prosper while those that fail to do so will stagnate. With regard to this point, the experiences of Argentina, Venezuela, Japan, and Hong Kong are instructive. As Exhibit 7 illustrates, in 1960 the per capita incomes of Japan and Hong Kong were only two-thirds to three-fourths as large as those of Argentina and Venezuela. By 1990, however, the situation was dramatically different. Adjusted for inflation, the 1990 per capita incomes of Argentina and Venezuela were only slightly greater than their 1960 level. The economies of these countries stagnated during the 1960–1990 period. In contrast, the inflation-adjusted per capita incomes of Japan and Hong Kong increased by more than fivefold during the same period. By 1990, the per capita incomes of Japan and Hong Kong were approximately three times greater than those of Argentina and Venezuela.

Exhibit 7: The Real Per Capita Income of Argentina, Venezuela, Japan, and Hong Kong—1960 and 1990

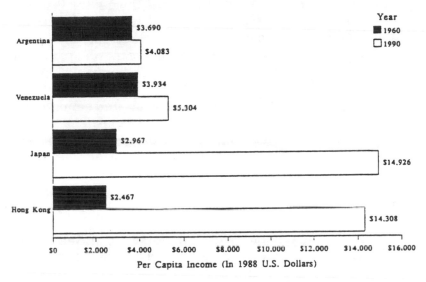

Per Capita Income (In 1988 U.S. Dollars)

Source: Robert Summers and Alan Heston, "The Penn World Table (Mark 5): An Expanded Set of International Comparisons, 1950–1988," *Quarterly Journal of Economics* (May 1991). The "purchasing power parity method" was used to convert to the U.S. dollar. The original 1988 data were updated to 1990 by the authors.

These data reveal a great deal about economic prosperity. First, they illustrate that natural resource abundance is neither a necessary nor a sufficient condition for economic prosperity. Japan has few natural resources and it imports almost all of its industrial energy supply. Hong Kong has practically no raw materials, very little fertile soil, and no domestic sources of energy. Yet both are prosperous. In contrast, Venezuela is one of the most oil-rich countries in the world, while Argentina has a great deal of fertile land and several other natural resources. Natural resources can help promote economic prosperity, but clearly they are not the key. If they were, Japan and Hong Kong would be poor, while Argentina and Venezuela would be rich.

Second, Exhibit 7 also illustrates the limitations of advanced technology as a source of economic growth. Clearly, improvements in technology have dramatically enhanced our ability to produce goods during the last 250 years. The substitution of power-driven machines for human labor, the development of miracle grains, fertilizers, new sources of energy, and improvements in transportation and communication have transformed the way of life in North America, Europe, Oceania, and Japan. Less-developed countries, however, can borrow and emulate the proven technologies of the developed countries. This should make it easier for them to grow and prosper. If technology were the primary factor limiting the creation of wealth, the economic well being of people in less-developed nations would be improving rapidly. Unfortunately, this is not the case.

Why did the economies of Japan and Hong Kong grow rapidly, while Argentina and Venezuela stagnated? Clearly, differences in economic organization are an important part of the answer. Our analysis indicates that securely defined property rights, low taxes, monetary stability, and reliance on markets are keys to economic progress. In general, Japan and Hong Kong followed this course during 1960-1990. In contrast, countries that restrict business and trade, impose high taxes, fix interest rates and other prices, and follow an inflationary monetary policy discourage productive activity and retard the efficient use of resources. In general, this has been the course followed by Argentina, Venezuela, and most of the other less-developed countries in recent decades.

Sound economic organization is the key to economic prosperity. Countries that adopt policies that encourage the creation of wealth will prosper, while those that fail to do so will continue to stagnate. This is true for both wealthy industrial nations and poor developing countries. The future prosperity of both is directly related to the soundness of their economic organization. This is the central message of modern economics.

Endnotes

1.   Adam Smith, *An Inquiry into the Nature and Causes of the Wealth of Nations*, (1776; Cannan's ed., Chicago: University of Chicago Press, 1976), p. 477.

2.   Henry Hazlitt, *Economics in One Lesson*, (New Rochelle: Arlington House, 1979), p. 103.

3.   Assar Lindbeck, *The Political Economy of the New Left, 1970* (New York: Harper and Row, 1972), p. 39.

4.   The conservation function of private ownership is also illustrated by examining alternative property right systems that are applied to animals. Animals like cattle, horses, llama, turkeys, and ostriches that are privately owned are conserved for the future. In contrast, the absence of private ownership has led to the excessive exploitation of animals like the buffalo, whale, and beaver. Contrasting approaches to the conservation of elephants in Africa also provides instructive evidence on the importance of private ownership. In Kenya, elephants roam unowned on unfenced terrain. The Kenyan government tries to protect elephants from poachers seeking valuable ivory by banning all commercial use of the elephant except tourism. In the decade that this policy has been in effect, the Kenyan elephant population has declined from 65,000 to 19,000. Other Eastern and Central African countries that have followed this approach have experienced a similar decline in the size of their elephant population. In contrast, Zimbabwe allows the open sale of elephant ivory and hides, but provides local people on whose land the elephant roams with rights of private ownership. Since assigning private ownership rights to elephants, Zimbabwe has seen its elephant population grow from 30,000 to 43,000. Elephant populations in the countries adopting a similar approach—Botswana, South Africa, Malawi, and Namibia—are also increasing. See Randy Simmons and Urs Kreuter, "Herd Mentality: Banning Ivory Sales Is No Way to Save the Elephant," *Policy Review* (Fall 1989), pp. 46-49, for additional details on this topic.

5.   The empirical evidence indicates that, adjusted for inflation, the prices of most natural resources have actually been falling for decades, and in most cases, for centuries. The classic study of Harold Barnett and Chandler Morris, *Scarcity and Growth: The Economics of Natural Resource Availability*, (Baltimore: The Johns Hopkins University Press, 1963) illustrates this point. Updates and extensions of this work indicate that resource

113

prices are continuing to decline. In 1980 economist Julian Simon bet doomsday environmentalist Paul Ehrlich that the inflation-adjusted price of any five natural resources of Ehrlich's choosing would decline during the 1980s. In fact, the prices of all five of the resources chosen by Ehrlich declined and Simon won the highly publicized bet. A recent study found that of 38 major natural resources, only two (manganese and zinc) increased in price (after adjustment for inflation) during the 1980s. See Stephen Moore, "So Much for 'Scarce Resources'," *Public Interest* (Winter 1992).

6.   Milton Friedman, "Economic Freedom, Human Freedom, Political Freedom," lecture delivered November 1, 1991 at California State University, Hayward. A booklet containing the lecture is available from the Smith Center for Private Enterprise Studies of California State University, Hayward.

7.   Clair Wilcox, *Competition and Monopoly in American Industry, Monograph no. 21*, Temporary National Economic Committee, Investigation of Concentration of Economic Power, 76th Congress, 3rd Session (Washington, DC: U.S. Government Printing Office, 1940).

8.   Adam Smith, *An Inquiry into the Nature and Causes of the Wealth of Nations*, p. 18.

9.   Henry George, *Protection or Free Trade* (1886, reprinted edition, New York: Robert Schalkenbach Foundation, 1980), p. 47.

10.   The principle that productive projects generate the potential for political unanimity was initially articulated by Swedish economist Knut Wicksell in 1896. See Wicksell, "A New Principle of Just Taxation," in James Gwartney and Richard Wagner (eds), *Public Choice and Constitutional Economics* (Greenwich: JAI Press, Inc., 1988). Nobel laureate James Buchanan has stated that Wicksell's work provided him with the insights that led to his major role in the development of modern public choice theory.

11.   Quotation is from *The Wall Street Journal*, December 16, 1983.

12.   As E. C. Pasour, Jr., of North Carolina State University, has pointed out to the authors, the federal "dinner check" analogy can be carried one step further. Suppose the check is to be divided evenly among the large group, but the ordering will be done by committee so there will be separate committees for

drinks, appetizers, entrees, salads, and desserts. Since each person can serve on the committees of his (or her) choice, lushes will end up on the drinks committee, vegetarians on the salad committee, sweet-tooths on the dessert committee, and so on. This arrangement further exacerbates the tendency toward over-ordering and over-spending. The arrangement just described closely resembles the committee structure of the U.S. Congress.

13. James R. Schlesinger, "Systems Analysis and the Political Process," *Journal of Law and Economics*, (October 1968), p. 281.

14. See Richard Epstein, *Takings: Private Property and the Power of Eminent Domain*, (Cambridge: Harvard University Press, 1985) for a comprehensive analysis of this point.

15. See James Gwartney and Richard Stroup, "Transfers, Equality, and the Limits of Public Policy," *Cato Journal*, (Spring/Summer 1986) for a detailed analysis of this issue.

16. Adam Smith, *The Theory of Moral Sentiments*, (1759; New York: A. M. Kelley, 1966).

17. Walter Lippmann, *The Good Society*, (New York: Grosset and Dunlop, 1956), p. 38.

18. Points (b) and (c) are borrowed from Milton and Rose Friedman, *Free to Choose*, (New York: Harcourt Brace Jovanovich, 1980). See particularly chapter 10.

19. Here it is important to distinguish between licensing and certification. Licensing requirements prohibit the practice of an occupation or profession without the permission of the state. They are a clear restraint on trade. In contrast, certification merely requires one to supply customers with information (for example, tests passed or educational levels achieved). As long as the certification is merely informational, it would not be prohibited by this amendment.

Suggested Additional Readings

Richard A. Epstein, *Takings: Private Property and the Power of Eminent Domain* (Cambridge: Harvard University Press, 1985).

Milton and Rose Friedman, *Free to Choose* (New York: Harcourt Brace Jovanovich, 1980).

Nathan Rosenberg and L.E. Birdzell Jr., *How the West Grew Rich* (New York: Basic Books, 1986).

Additional books by Gwartney and Stroup

For more thorough coverage of the principles outlined in this book, see James D. Gwartney and Richard L. Stroup's, *Economics: Private and Public Choice, 6th edition,* 1992 (ISBN 0-15-518921-2) and *Introduction to Economics: The Wealth and Poverty of Nations, 1st edition,* 1994 (ISBN 0-03-098291-X). Both are published by the Dryden Press, a division of Harcourt Brace & Company.

About The Authors

James D. Gwartney is a Professor of Economics and Policy Sciences at Florida State University and a Research Associate of the James Madison Institute. He received his Ph.D. in Economics from the University of Washington in 1970. He has published numerous articles in professional journals of economics, primarily in the areas of taxation, public choice and labor economics. His popular writings have appeared in many newspapers including the *New York Times* and *The Wall Street Journal*.

Richard L. Stroup is a Professor of Economics at Montana State University and a Senior Associate of the Political Economy Research Center. He received his Ph.D. from the University of Washington in 1970 and was the Director of the Office of Policy Analysis at U.S. Department of Interior during 1982-1984. Widely published in the areas of natural resources and environmental economics, he has been a major force in the development of the approach to resource problems known as free market environmentalism. His recent research has focused on alternative institutional arrangements for dealing with environmental risk.

Professors Gwartney and Stroup are both members of the Mont Pelerin Society, an international organization of economists. They are the coauthors of *Economics: Private and Public Choice, 6th edition.* (Harcourt Brace Jovanovich, 1992), a widely used college level economics text and *Introductory Economics: The Wealth and Poverty of Nations* which is scheduled for publication in 1994.

What Others Are Saying About This Book...

"Seldom does the title of a book tell the truth about its contents. This one does. Gwartney and Stroup have managed to bring down to earth the stratospheric language of academics, and have brought out of the dark the forgotten links between the economic order and the political system."

Juan F. Bendfeldt
Professor of Economics
Universidad Francisco Marroquin
Guatemala

"This book will be quite useful both to students and to professors—even those who already know most of its content—because it is unusually well structured. It integrates the modern treatment of transactions costs and public choice with traditional economic insights."

Henri LePage
Institute Euro '92
Paris, France

"Economics is interesting, useful, a lot of fun. Gwartney and Stroup have proven this in their easily understood mini-text that's destined to occupy a dedicated space on the bookshelves of students, businessmen, informed citizens, and hopefully, those politicians who say they care about America's prosperity."

Walter E. Williams
John M. Olin Distinguished
Professor of Economics
George Mason University

"With elegance and clarity, Gwartney and Stroup show that government meddling in the peaceful affairs of its citizens destroys rather than creates the prosperity politicians promise. Their solution? An Economic Bill of Rights to restrain the voracious appetite of special interests for more power and money."

Albert H. Zlabinger
Vienna, Austria

"Gwartney and Stroup have done a marvelous job. They have stripped economics of its jargon and graphs. Lay-readers now have a non-technical explanation of the processes that generate wealth and the destructive effects of government intervention. Gwartney and Stroup's book will especially benefit business people and journalists. Politicians of all stripes should definitely read it."

Alan Gibbs, Chairman
Gibbs Securities Ltd.
Auckland, New Zealand

"This book is the concentrated essence of economic enlightenment on how and why men and women are productive in markets but destructive in government, condensed into 100 pages of plain English for the citizen, the taxpayer, and the voter."

Arthur Seldon, Founder President
Institute of Economic Affairs
London, England

"If officials in Washington would follow the principles so concisely presented in this book, we could avoid the economic policy mistakes that so often produce political business cycles."

Manley Johnson, former
Vice-chairman, Board of Governors
of the Federal Reserve System

"This book contains powerful and revolutionary ideas that every person who is free, or longs to be, should know and understand."

Phil Gramm
U.S. Senator – Texas

"If you are looking for a lean and clean book on economics—a basic primer for keeping clear the main ideas—this may be the best you'll find. It sticks to the basics, and explains them with common sense and in plain English. It will leave you wishing that everyone really *did* know at least these basics."

Michael Novak
American Enterprise Institute